I0170324

What Works

Three Great Truths

The White Feather Press

O.A. Bud Ham

© 2015 O.A. Bud Ham
All rights reserved. Printed in the United States of America.
No part of this book may be used or reproduced in any form
without the written permission of The White Feather Press.
2697 South Macon Court Aurora, Colorado 80014

First edition
First Printing, 2015

ILLUSTRATIONS: Retta Va Springer
BOOK DESIGN: Bob Schram, Bookends

ISBN 978-0-9646397-5-1

Acknowledgments

I t is with great thanks and respect that I thank those who have contributed to the completion of this book. I consider this book as a significant part of my mission.

To: REVEREND DAVID MORRISSEY for helping me more clearly understand *A Course In Miracles* and introducing me to *The Way of Mastery*.

To: AUTHOR PEG BRANTLEY for huge contributions to the writing quality and her help in bringing this book to completion.

To: BOB SCHRAM, OWNER OF BOOKENDS DESIGN for inspiration and professional guidance in publishing.

To: FAMILY AND FRIENDS, including James Callender for suggestions to increase clarity and relevance of content.

To: RETTA VA SPRINGER for the cover and enhancement drawings.

D e d i c a t i o n

I dedicate this book to my wife and Soul mate Judy,
loving friends, and our family.
They helped me understand there is a difference
between Preaching and Teaching.

–BUD HAM

Contents

WHAT WORKS:
THREE GREAT TRUTHS

This book is a compendium of my Truths.
Please be mindful that my truths
might not be your truths.
If that be so, neither is wrong—just different.

MY MISSION

To contribute as much as I can to the quality of life and mission fulfillment of as many people as possible by raising spiritual awareness and encouraging open-minded spiritual exploration.

IN MY LIFE I HAVE BEEN BLESSED by many mentors who have helped me know what works. Without question, what has worked for me, and has had the greatest impact on my quality of life and mission fulfillment is the study of two books: *A Course in Miracles (ACIM)* and *The Way of Mastery (TWOM)*. This writing explores these books in great detail. Contact information:

A Course in Miracles
Published by the Foundation for Inner Peace
P. O. Box 598
Mill Valley, CA 94942
www.acim.org

The Way of Mastery
Published by Shanti Christo Foundation
P. O. Box 3232
Ashland, OR 97520
www.shantichristo.org

OUR CHANGING WORLD

In many respects the world is a very different place than it was when I finished writing my first book, *You Are in the Right Place* in 1995 and the second one, *Changing Places to Another Right Place* published in 2005.

One motivation for writing both books was to help clarify my own thoughts. An equally important motivation was to make a contribution to humankind's progress toward a happier and more peaceful and harmonious life as individuals and thus make the world a better place. I am satisfied there was at least some contribution from both books.

During the first few months, after the release of *You Are in the Right Place,* four people came to me and said the book had saved their lives. Of course I never probed for more information. Two of them said they had planned their suicides and changed their minds after reading the book. Several people told me *Changing Places to Another Right Place* had eased the pain of a difficult divorce. Still others have been motivated to communicate with Spirit through meditation, followed by writing whatever words come to their consciousness.

What is the purpose of this book?

To awaken or re-awaken the possibility in our thinking of the existence of mystical, super-natural Guides and Guardian Angels and the potential of their help.

To "know" (stronger than belief) that my life experiences, including: health; happiness; prosperity and love-based relationships, is the direct result of decisions I made in the past—*"I am responsible!"*

To encourage removal of fear-based, religious blinders to expand our awareness.

To enhance the acceptance of the personal power that is inherent in every human being. The power to make positive changes in our thinking and therefore our lives.

To advance thinking that can lead us to a one-to-one relationship with God that is founded on love and completely without fear.

To promote the idea that each of us has his or her path to spiritual enlightenment that is unique—different from anyone else's who has ever lived—and that everyone who seeks peace through love-based oneness with God will find it.

To elevate the consciousness of as many people as possible, as early in our lives as possible, to accept that God is our best friend. And, as with all best friends, our wish is His command, on His time table, as long as it brings no harm to anyone.

To further advance the concepts:
- We are all one.
- There is enough of everything.
- There is nothing we must do to have God's love—it is ours unconditionally—no matter what we do.

To encourage readers to experiment, to **test,** Spirituality. For example, test your personal ability to dialogue with God, especially when stressed—try it, you have nothing to lose! The simple four step process:
- *What is the truth here Father?*
- *What is in the best interest of all concerned?*
- *Shut up and listen!*
- *Pay attention to feelings and be patient.*

An Overview of the Current
Spiritual Beliefs of the Author

NOTE: My life's journey and history of religious/spiritual beliefs is available in two other books; *You are in the Right Place* and *Changing Places to Another Right Place*

I willingly share the following intensely personal information with any reader who is interested. It could be useful to help you understand the content of this book. I have no need to challenge the beliefs of others or to defend my own. Any review of my spiritual beliefs must be dated because I am committed to being a continuous student. My current beliefs include but are not limited to the following:

✧ At any point in time, it does not matter what life path we are on—spiritual or non-spiritual—or how it evolves, **we are always in the right place.**

✧ Forgiveness of others and our self is necessary for personal peace.

✧ Fear is an unnecessary ego-based emotion that with God's help we can eliminate from our lives.

✧ The countless turning points in our lives were not just "OK" they were perfect.

✧ In the past few years I have read Neale Donald Walsch's books *Conversations with God, books 1, 2, and 3; Friendship with God; Communion with God* and *New Revelations.* Each time I re-read these books or listen to them on tape I experience a higher level of peace and well being.

✧ I strongly endorse the book and audio recordings of Deepak Chopra's book *The Seven Spiritual Laws of Success.*

✧ In studying Deepak Chopra's book *How to Know God* I have identified:
  - Where I think I am in knowing God. It is satisfying and inspiring.
  - Every good and loving work I do, I co-create with God.
    - Of myself I can do nothing. The Father working through me and my brothers and sisters accomplishes all good things.
  - Our lives change in direct proportion to our love-based decision making.
    - Ego-based decisions are fear-based and **cannot serve us well.**

✧ I have read *The Autobiography of a Yogi* by Paramahansa Yogananda. I loved the emphasis on inclusion of all spiritual paths and the Hindu philosophy of non-violence. It has increased my interest in Eastern philosophy. I am impressed with the credence Buddhists and Hindu holy men and women give to Jesus and his teaching. I believe it is to the advantage of Christians and people of other faiths to reciprocate.

✧ Several of my spiritual brothers have been attending retreats and experiencing Siddha Yoga. A part of the teaching of most Eastern spiritual philosophies is the importance of a personal teacher or "guru." I am directed to welcome any information, from any love-based source, that can contribute to my spiritual growth.

✧ After several years of intense but intermittent study of *A Course in Miracles* I have concluded that it is, at this time, my primary path of spiritual study. My introduction and study of the book *The Way of Mastery, (TWOM)* has significantly furthered my understanding of *A Course in Miracles, (ACIM)*. Both books were dictated by Jeshua ben Joseph (Jesus).

✧ A thorough understanding of Jesus' teaching, *"Cast your bread on the waters and it will be returned to you multiplied"* puts us in direct and complete control of our future. It is the Christian statement of karma—*you will receive whatever you give away.*

- If you want respect, give respect to others.
- If you want cooperation, be cooperative.
- If you want recognition, give recognition.
- If you want others to listen to you, listen to them.
- If you want more love, give more love.
- If you want more money, take all you can spare, with love in your heart and without discrimination, give it to anyone who needs it more than you.
- If you want people to deal fairly with you and to treat you by the Golden Rule adopt it as your primary guiding principle.
- It is incongruent not to *do unto yourself* as you would do unto others or have others do unto you.
- The reciprocal of the above eight items is also true.

✧ Spiritual laws are irrefutable. To use them as management principles in our personal, professional and business lives is more than prudent—it is pure genius.

✧ To live stress free I recommit each morning to fulfill my part of God's Plan this day. (ACIM Workbook lesson #98.)

✧ To increase quality of life use Spiritual Guidance moment to moment—not just during crisis.

**Before the book begins in earnest,
I choose to share the following story:**

THE GAME WARDENS

COMPASSION; noun, SYMPATHY also charity, clemency, benevolence, humaneness. Webster's Thesaurus.
A single act of love-based compassion can have a positive effect on the lives of countless people over a period of many, many years.

I grew up hearing the stories about how difficult life was during the winter of 1931–1932—caused by the Great Depression. At that time my family was buying a ranch in the Roaring Fork River Valley near Carbondale, Colorado. My dad and my grandfather sold all of their livestock trying unsuccessfully to meet their financial obligations.

One of my dad's favorite stories of events during this difficult time was of him shooting six deer that winter with seven bullets fired from my grandpa's .303 British bolt action rifle—and how they drained beaver ponds for trout to vary the diet of venison and potatoes. The bank foreclosed the ranch in September, 1932, shortly after I was born. The families moved back to what we knew as "the home place" in the Arkansas River Valley of Southern Colorado.

FLORENCE, COLORADO The Great Depression ended slowly in our small Southern Colorado town. Almost every family had a garden plot, a couple of fruit trees, a chicken house and a few rabbit hutches. One way to have food for the table was to raise your own. And of course, there was a weekly distribution at the welfare station of what was referred to as "commodities"—powdered eggs and milk, flour, cheese, and any surplus fruit or vegetables.

The other source of food was hunting and fishing. We hunted jack rabbits and cotton tails, pheasants, quail and ducks, doves and deer.

Fishing was for trout, river chubs, white suckers and an occasional carp. Yes, we did eat all of them! My mom would grind up the cleaned and skinned carp, suckers and chubs—bones included; mix the ground fish with cracker crumbs, eggs and various spices and make fish patties. They were delicious.

Mr. Ireland

My first encounter with a game warden was in 1940. I was about eight years old. His last name was Ireland. Trout fishing regulations at that time in Colorado were 20 fish per day or 10 pounds and one fish. All trout had to be at least 7 inches long. My father carved a notch in the cork handle of my fly rod 7 inches from the end—my measuring tool. Chubs and suckers didn't have a size limit and didn't count in the bag limit.

My dad, my grandpa, an uncle and I were fishing one Sunday west of Canon City on the Arkansas River during the spring runoff. The cloudy water made it impossible for me to fish with flies and my bait was referred to by my father as "garden hackle"—worms.

When Mr. Ireland checked my creel two of the three trout in it were about an eighth of an inch short of 7 inches. He laid the three trout on a flat rock with great deliberateness. He quietly looked at the fish and I was about to panic when he said, "These two have dried out and shrunk a bit since you caught them. I suggest that in the future you keep some wet grass in your creel so that won't happen again. And remember the regulation says 7 inches." My panic subsided and my dad shook his hand.

Sometime after that episode Mr. Ireland retired and he was replaced by a man in his 60s—Mr. J.C. Malloy—a man whom we shall get to know better!

A RITE OF PASSAGE

I was permitted to start hunting after my 12th birthday. My father presented me with the Page-Lewis Arms Co. single shot, .22 rifle. I had been permitted to shoot previously—but under close supervision. Now I was allowed to hunt by myself. It was a very proud day when I returned home from a solo Saturday morning hunt with two cotton tail rabbits.

That same Fall, 1944, an elderly neighbor visited with my dad and me one afternoon and said there were too many muskrats and skunks in our area and he volunteered to teach me how to trap them.

I had a few dollars from working on neighbor's farms that summer and on Mr. Montgomery's instruction I ordered a dozen size1/2 Onieda-Victor single spring traps and two size 1 traps with double springs for skunks. I ordered the traps from a Montgomery-Ward Co. catalogue. I was so excited I could hardly sleep nights until after the first frost when Monty allowed that fur would now be prime. It was indeed a memorable, life-changing time in my life.

A fur buyer came through our area just before Christmas. Monty just beamed when the buyer paid me 25 dollars (a small fortune in 1944) for a dozen muskrats and two skunk pelts. His take was much larger.

Before I started trapping my father and my grandfather both came to me, separately, to voice their opinions about me trapping. They said it was well and good that I was going to be a trapper but I shouldn't forget I had morning and evening farm chores to do. And they both said, with great emphasis, that in addition I must check my traps twice a day to reduce the suffering of the trapped animals.

When I was 14 I decided to expand my trapping territory. After two seasons of trapping on irrigation canals, practically in our back yard, I decided to include a stretch of the Arkansas River and a nearby swamp. This longer trap line required more time.

To check my traps, complete my farm chores and still get to school on time required me to start my day at 4:00 AM and check my traps with a flash light.

That was when my mother "put her foot down" and said I had to have a trapping partner. She was concerned for my safety. That was a good decision— but that's another story—this one is about game wardens.

J. C. MALLOY

He was a portly man, I would guess in his mid-sixties; about six feet tall; grey hair and mustache; thick glasses; and he wore suspenders. His vehicle was a black, 1937 Chevrolet coup. Every encounter I had with him happened at the same place—the end of the dirt road that ran by our small farm and dead ended about a half mile away at the river.

The first time I encountered him my trapping partner, Jimmy Bassett and I were returning from a fruitless rabbit hunt. We each had a single shot .22 rifle. The trees, bushes and other vegetation at the end of the road made it almost impossible to see a vehicle from any distance. He startled us as he stepped out of the bushes saying, "Howdy boys! How was he hunt?"

After a bit of small talk he asked if we had the box our bullets came in. I instantly produced one. He took it and opened the flap, handed it back to me and said, "What does that say?"

I quickly responded by reading aloud, "Dangerous within one mile."

Mr. Malloy said, "That's right and I don't ever want to see you shoot those guns in the air."

Then he added as he turned on his heel and left, *"I'd rather see you here than in a pool hall."*

SUBSEQUENT ENCOUNTERS

The river bottom was thickly forested with cottonwood trees—great small game habitat. That, and rights of way for irrigation canals and abandoned railroad lines in Fremont County provided great cover for Chinese ring neck pheasants.

The Colorado Game and Fish Department stocked the birds in the late 1930s but they never opened a hunting season for them. The semi-arid foothills south of town provided equally good habitat for scaled quail. But in the 1940s there was no open season on quail either.

When I was 14 my grandfather presented me with a family heirloom—a model 1894 Marlin, 12 gauge pump shotgun. He bought the gun new in 1897 for $26.00. The shotgun greatly improved my ability to bring home game for the family to eat.

A typical Saturday for me and my partner during the fall and winter began in the early morning, just after farm chores. I would leave home with a .22 caliber pistol and the Marlin shotgun. I carried the pistol to dispatch any skunk that we might have caught. One of the main activities was to move our muskrat traps to a fresh area—in the hope of increasing our take. Then we would spend the rest of the day hunting—any small game that was edible—ducks, rabbits, quail or pheasants.

I also carried the shotgun on my daily trap checking. I was frequently able to bring down a duck or a pheasant to contribute to the family larder.

A number of times in my mid teen-age years I encountered Mr. Malloy. On some of these occasions I could have been arrested for illegal possession of small game. Once I had nine quail zipped up inside my jacket, another time I had two mallards, again inside my jacket. Both of these times there were blood soaked spots showing through the front of my jacket.

At each encounter we made a little small talk, none of which I remember. But I shall always remember what he said each time as we parted: *"I'd rather see you here than in a pool hall!"*

The most memorable encounter happened one day when I had an illegal pheasant stuffed in my jacket. He asked me if I would like a ride home. I didn't want to—but I said yes. He knew exactly where I lived and he was driving at least 40 miles an hour as we sped past our drive way. I was in a complete speechless panic. I was sure we were headed right for the county jail! He looked at me and burst out laughing as he stopped the car. Before the car had completely stopped I jumped out and ran for home. I clearly remember hearing his laughter.

Mr. Malloy was known as one of the state of Colorado's most respected game wardens. It was said that he would arrest his own mother if she was a poacher. But he wouldn't arrest a kid!

I never did become one of the pool hall group. I shall be forever grateful for Mr. Malloy's compassion.

NOTE: I have been an ardent outdoorsman, hunter and fisherman for more than 70 years. Please know that I am a dedicated advocate of obeying game laws.

WHAT WORKS:
THREE GREAT TRUTHS

To expect a different outcome without changing
the input is insanity. Said another way;
"If what you have been doing is not working,
more of the same will not work either."
–ANONYMOUS

LET US BEGIN with what might be the greatest and
most difficult change in our thinking, and therefore our behavior—giving up judgment. It has long
been said by sages and other wise spiritual teachers
that we are incapable of making accurate judgments
(right or wrong; good or bad) about people, events
or situations. The Wise Ones tell us to do so with
usefulness and accuracy we need to have all of the
facts, almost surely impossible. And, if that were
not difficult enough, they help us understand that to
make accurate judgments we would need to know
the impact of the behavior, item or event on all
people for all time—definitely impossible.

Therefore let us not become ensnared in the ego motivated trap of judging an event or person as "right" or "wrong"—"good" or "bad" and concern ourselves only with **WHAT WORKS!**

Through the ages spiritual prognosticators have told us of the coming Age of Aquarius—a time of peace and prosperity. Recent events have suggested to many wise thinkers that the world in now in a state of transition toward that more desirable way of being. I am an optimist and I choose to accept this line of thinking. *The purpose of this book is to help as many people as possible become contributors to this more desirable way of thinking and thusly, being.*

Chapter One

EVOLVING OUR
BELIEF SYSTEMS

T HERE IS AN AWESOME ORDERLINESS in the universe. Understanding of the regularity in the travel of the planets; the phases of the moon and the predictability of the tides, have come from the study and agreement of great and dedicated minds. My thinking leads me to believe that there is also purpose in the universe. If that is so, the next question people want answered is, *"What is my purpose?"* This, of course, requires spiritual investigation.

It occurs to me, if I can determine what works in my life and what doesn't, I shall be led to clarification of my purpose. It is to my obvious benefit to be aware of what doesn't work, and to have the discipline to avoid self-defeating activities. I have long believed that there are irrefutable, natural laws in the universe. My interest has been to develop an awareness of the plethora of variables affecting outcomes.

The Wise Ones have clearly advised to "Follow our heart" or as the beloved teacher/philosopher Joseph Campbell taught us, *"Follow your bliss."*

Could it be that is how God talks to us? My experience strongly suggests that it is. For me, *it works!*

FULFILLING OUR NEEDS

To be effective in the world we must make plans. Yet, it is to our distinct advantage not to become too attached to predetermined outcomes. We often find that the expected achievement does not resolve the need that was expected from the achievement of that goal. There is an ancient Jewish proverb that states: *"Men plan and God laughs."* We cannot know, with certainty, what is best for us or all of the other people that an outcome will affect. When the satisfaction resulting from an outcome is not what we thought it would be, or the one we expected, doubt often creeps into our thinking.

DIVINE INTERVENTION

In a Gallop Poll of a few years ago it was established that more than 95% of people in the United States have a belief in God. Of this 95% most of them also believe that there has been divine intervention in their lives. These individuals have a "resource" that non-believers appear not to have.

Oh, they have it alright, but since they are unaware of the resource they do not utilize it. For all of us, there are those times when events aren't happening to our liking and doubt is making us fearful and therefore unhappy.

Those with the spiritual resource are well advised to follow the admonition of the Sage, Obi Wan Kenobi to Luke Skywalker in the first Star Wars movie. When Luke Skywalker was about to lose his life in a fight to the finish with an alien invader the Sage said to him, *"Luke, trust the Force."* As you know, Luke won!

TESTING SPIRITUALITY

In our culture we "test" things when there is doubt about the outcome. In my opinion it is perfectly OK to test spirituality to see if it "works." If you continue to find the content of this book interesting and potentially useful you will be introduced to several opportunities to personally conduct tests or exercises to see what works for you. **These tests take only a small amount of time and energy and may contribute immeasurably to your quality of life. Only you can decide if a spiritual belief, a concept or an activity is useful to you.**

THE BEST "ONE LINER" I'VE EVER HEARD

A few years ago I had the great opportunity to work with a PhD psychologist who was also an ordained Lutheran minister, Dr. Charles Sorenson. He and I were facilitating a series of team-building and marketing workshops for several dental practices in Grand Junction, Colorado.

After a successful workshop we were enjoying an evening walk. He said that a recent Gallop poll found that 95% of Americans believe in God and that a great majority also believe that God has intervened in their lives. He then said; "If those people take one more step on the spiritual path they will never work again." I excitedly responded by saying, "Tell me more!" He then said; **"If work becomes part of your worship you will never work again."**

I quit work more than 35 years ago!

FOUNDATIONAL INFORMATION

The idea that anyone can do a comprehensive job of identifying what doesn't work and what does work is ludicrous and one holding that position might be identified as arrogant. Yet, if we can identify a partial and useful list of desirable and acceptable foundational concepts that can add to the clarification of our purpose in life the list can help us.

The following concepts and philosophical positions, to be sure are incomplete but hopefully can provide a starting point for us as individuals to identify what works in our lives and "do" more of that.

THREE GREAT TRUTHS

In song and prose and poetry Seekers have asked the question throughout history, *"What is truth?"* I wish I could say what truth is for you, of course I cannot. It is sometimes difficult, and often impossible for me to say what truth is for me. Yet, I do believe that if one earnestly seeks truth, works at it long enough, and is open to guidance, our personal list of truths expands. This process also clarifies another truth—*My truth may not be your truth!* I share my truths with you, not to suggest that they should become yours, only that they might serve you also.

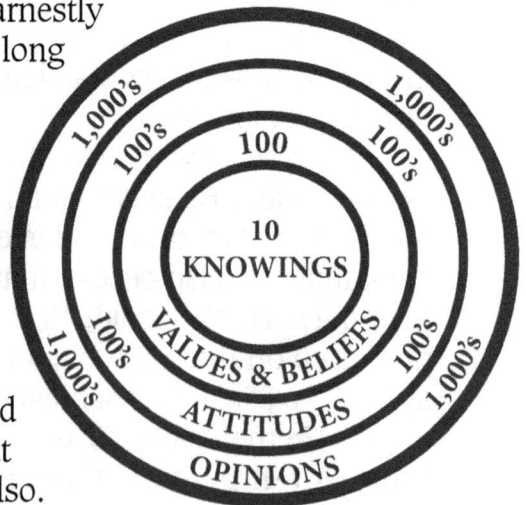

FIRST GREAT TRUTH

You will become what you think.

✧ If you think fearful thoughts you will become frightened.

✧ If your thoughts dwell on illness you will become sick.

✧ If you think peaceful thoughts you will become a serene person.

✧ If you think loving thoughts you become a warm, caring person.

✧ If you think hateful thoughts you become a mean-spirited person.

Let us be reminded of another great axiom from The Wise Ones: *"The thought is father of the deed."* It is to our distinct advantage to learn the lessons unpleasant events of our past can teach us. If we do indeed learn from an event it becomes a gift rather than a burden. If, after the learning, we release the event and refuse to dwell on it, it will not negatively influence our future. To fully enjoy the gift from the learning it is imperative that we forgive others **and ourselves** for any contributions we may have made to what might have been an unpleasant or painful event.

All of us have ugly, mean-spirited thoughts from time to time— **but we can choose not to entertain them and we can replace them!—*"I can choose again!"***

Becoming what we think is the *Law of Attraction* manifested. The law states: *We attract to ourselves that which we love or that which we fear or hate. The "attractant" is our thought energy—the message is:* **Don't put your thought energy into something you don't want!**

SECOND GREAT TRUTH

Whatever you want in life, give it away.

✧ If you want respect, give respect.

✧ If you want cooperation, give cooperation.

✧ If you want people to listen to you, listen to them.

✧ If you want more love, give more love away.

✧ If you want more money, take all you can spare and without discrimination give it to anyone who needs it more than you do.

✧ If you have something you can't give away, you don't own it, it owns you.

✧ To give anything away opens the channel for the inflow of much more of the same.

The ancient pronouncements, "as you sow, so shall you reap" and "cast your bread on the water and it will be returned multiplied," attest to this very simple law of *cause and effect.*

Do you want more love in your life? No one ever has too much! We know the wealthiest person in the world cannot buy love! The most powerful person in the world cannot command it. Yet, if we cast love on the water we can surely expect it will be returned multiplied.

The same principle holds true for mean-spirited acts! Perhaps we should pity any person, as they "shoot themselves in the foot." If we entertain fear-based, mean-spirited thoughts that lead to mean-spirited behavior we have "cast it on the water" and we are injuring ourselves because it will be returned.

The Buddhists teach that everything in life cycles. My understanding is that whatever we do in thought, word, or deed we "put it on the wheel." The wheel cycles and returns to us—maybe it is a small wheel and that which we put on it this morning comes back to us in the afternoon. Or, maybe it is a gigantic wheel that goes out into the cosmos and returns to us much, much later—but it does return.

THIRD GREAT TRUTH

We are in control of our own destiny.

If we accept and practice the first two Great Truths we can ignore fate and luck and accept that where I am today is a result of my past thoughts and actions. We cannot change our past. It does not exist—but if we do not release the past—especially the pain of the past—it will negatively influence our future.

To take positive control of the "NOW" is to claim control of our future. In Ekhart Tolle's book, *The Power of Now,* is the following wisdom, paraphrased a bit; "Whatever is happening in your life (pleasant or unpleasant) accept it as if you had planned it in every detail. Don't fear it, work with it not against it, and then, if it is possible and appropriate, take action. This will change your very life."

NOTE: The preceding is in the belief system of the author—greatly influenced by mentors such as Jesus, Tolle; Wayne Dyer; Deepak Chopra; Neil Donald Walsch; Dale Carnegie and others. As such I may view them differently in the future, yet please be assured they are "my truths" *("knowings")* as I see them now.

–BH

A BELIEF SYSTEM

Opinions; Attitudes; Beliefs; and Knowings

It is most appropriate for us to have *opinions* about anything we experience with our senses—we have many thousands of these. Some of these opinions receive more of our thoughts and develop into *attitudes,* perhaps a few hundred. Even fewer advance to the status of *beliefs and values,* perhaps a hundred or so. Some beliefs, probably just a few, can become *knowings.* Knowings are stronger than beliefs but they are not cast in stone. They are no longer part of my conscious seeking, yet they can change. It has taken me many years of mentoring, thought, experience and observation to "own" my knowings.

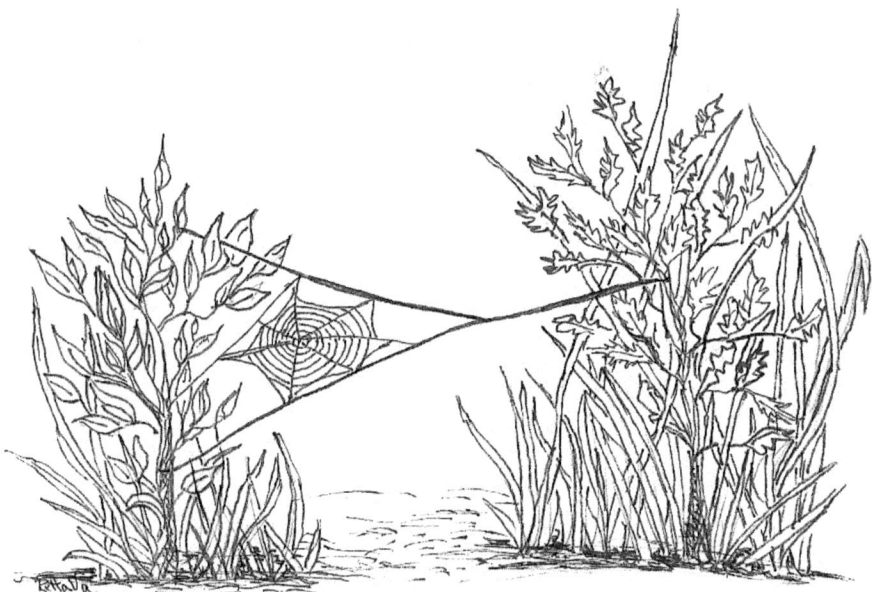

Chapter Two

USING OUR RESOURCES

If a person has a belief in a "Higher Power" or God, that person has a resource or "tool." There are those, of course, who do not know they have that resource. This book is for those who have and use that resource *OR* want to develop it. Exploring spirituality with an open mind can be life altering. Giving spirituality a fair trial by actually testing it is highly recommended. As suggested earlier, testing a spiritual principal is one of life's opportunities where there is the possibility of much to be gained and little or nothing to lose.

T HE VALUE OF *FAITH,* is just like any other value. The only way to truly own it is to carefully think it through, examine it, research it, perhaps discuss it with respected mentors, **and test it.** This is performing due diligence for one of the most important investments of our lives. When we decide to test a spiritual concept or a value and it measures up to rigorous testing, we might choose to own it. *If we do so it will then indeed be ours! It can become a* *"knowing" rather than a belief, and we will be much more likely to exert the energy and discipline to use it at every opportunity.*

A STUDY OF VALUES—VALUES DEFINED

Obtained from Avrom King

- ✧ A value is something we prize and cherish
- ✧ To be owned a value must be publicly acclaimed
- ✧ The unexamined value is not valued
- ✧ Examination requires freedom
- ✧ When the value changes the person changes
- ✧ A value not acted upon is not owned
- ✧ Values do not change under pressure
- ✧ No two people have exactly the same values

Owned Versus Imposed Values

Many defeated people arrive at their frustrating and unhappy state of life while trying to follow *imposed values*—values imposed on them by others, including parents, religious organizations, or other well-meaning people or groups. Many people in prisons and homeless centers began their path to unhappiness and hopeless frustration and dysfunction while trying to direct their lives by values they did not own. We may be intellectually aware of many values and if we own them we have greatly increased the probability of *living* (not violating) them.

As stated above, wise men have told us, "An unexamined value is not valued." When we violate a value because of low commitment, we are likely to suffer the twin demons of guilt and frustration, seriously eroding our feelings of self-worth. If we continue to violate the value we think is ours, one of two things is likely to happen:

1) We will discard the value and cease to be influenced by it.

OR

2) We will have some form of fear/guilt-based neurotic reaction.

Losers are very good at rationalizing their undesirable outcomes that they label as failures ("It wasn't my fault.") And they choose to become a victim. Let us remember a definition of rationalizing is: *To devise self-satisfying but incorrect reasons for one's behavior*. It is the opposite of accepting personal responsibility for our circumstances.

Even the least creative among us can find others, or situations beyond our control, on which to blame what we label a failure or an undesirable outcome. Almost invariably "losers" become victims and develop the "poor little old me" syndrome. It is important to note that only losers have failures—***when winners have undesirable outcomes they become "learning experiences"—stepping stones toward what will work! They ask the question, "What can I learn from this event?" Accepting this process changes a problem into a blessing!***

CORE VALUES

To be happy, healthy, successful and prosperous is not complicated. Yes it is simple, but for some, not easy. To achieve these four desirable states we must be true to ourselves through striving to live our value system—in particular our "core" or primary values. If a person diligently attempts to live her or his life by a set of "owned" core values it leads to acceptance of the greatest value of all—the value of faith, which includes, of course, faith in one's self.

For many years a favorite area of interest for me has been the study of values. I owe a lot of my understanding of this subject to the recently departed researcher/philosopher/consultant Avrom King. Research and our own experiences tell us that values do change from time to time—but not easily or rapidly. Sometimes they become so entrenched that they become habits to which we might no longer give conscious thought. Let us hope those are "good" habits— or as psychologist Dr. William Glasser called them, "positive addictions." **The only way they are changed is by changing our thoughts:**

❖ Our thoughts change when we have an open mind; receive new information (education); and then ***choose*** to think differently and thus behave differently!

❖ Learning happens when we test the new information, find it useful or not useful; clarify our thinking and values; and behave congruently.

❖ With this line of thinking it can be to our advantage to examine long entrenched values—asking the question, "Does this value serve me well at the present time?"

✧ The same can be asked of attitudes and opinions.

✧ An honest evaluation of this question eliminates
the cop-out position of, "That's just the way I am."
It can be thought of as more mature to think,
"Wherever I am, *I am there by choice* and I can
choose differently."

A few years ago I began the process of "boiling
down" a long list of values that I thought were
necessary for team members to share if they were
to become mission driven and true family or team
players. After considerable thought and discussion I
reduced a long "grocery list" of values to five. My son
Michael, who is also my consulting partner, caused
me to re-examine them and expand them with the
addition of *nurturing*. This addition considerably
increases the usefulness of the concept. Neither the
values nor the definitions are all inclusive by any
means—but they are a good starting point and I
believe these values are shared by the members of
almost all successful teams! They are as follows:

MORALITY

Morality can be defined as striving to live
by the highest mores of our society. A moral
society assures our freedom and our prosperity.
A moral person never does anything to intentionally hurt herself or himself or any other
person. This person strives to govern his or her
behavior in such a way that it has the greatest
possibility of contributing to the quality of his
or her own life, and the lives of others.

INTEGRITY

There are many definitions of integrity—I've never heard a bad one. I like to keep things simple, so when I heard the definition used by Angelis Arian (she is a spiritual and philosophical teacher and speaker) I instantly adopted it. It is: *Say what you will do and then do what you said you would.* Said another way, *"Walk your talk."*

Living with integrity includes keeping all of your promises, even those you made "off the cuff" with little or no thought. Yet, we are well advised to always retain the prerogative of changing our mind—the only constant in our world is change! If you do change your mind after having made a commitment, to maintain integrity, you must inform the person to whom you made the commitment.

NOTE: My memory has never been perfect—and is even less so now. To help me keep my promises I carry a "Plugger's" palm pilot—no batteries to go dead and no crystal to break—just a small, shirt-pocket sized note-book in which to make reminder notes. It works for me!

REVERENCE FOR LIFE

Every living thing is of value in and of itself. Even those who take the lives of animals to use their bodies for human consumption can do so with reverence for the animal. It is customary, in the practice of their spirituality, for American Indians to pray for the spirit of the animal they killed and to thank it for giving up its life to sustain theirs'.

If a person who does not have reverence for life becomes either angry or frustrated, that one is capable of great violence. We have experienced this in our society by wanton killing of innocent people. Many who have died had nothing to do with creating the frustration that triggered the violence.

Reverence for all life must be taught. Ideally, it is taught to children by the example of adults. People who are taught reverence can suffer great frustration and still not succumb to violence. Without reverence, frustrated children or adults can kill and be justified in their minds. That does not mean we should not spray the wasps on the porch, but it does mean we should not put the wasps to death without compassion and awareness that we are destroying life.

TOLERANCE

The opposite of tolerance is, of course, intolerance. Intolerance is fear-based and born of ignorance. Intolerance leads to judgment. Judgment leads to prejudice. One of the great teachers of the 20th century, psychologist Abraham Maslow, taught us:

"One of the least likely problems of a Self-actualized (very mature) *person is racial, religious, ethnic, gender or life-style prejudice."*

Let us keep in mind, without prejudice there would be no wars. In all wars the enemy is depicted as subhuman. We can all start being increasingly tolerant by accepting that everyone is in the right place for him or her. That is discernment, rather than judgment, it does not mean condoning. We are in different places, not right or wrong ones. We could all significantly benefit from considering the precept that we are all one—*"Anything I do for you, I do for me. Likewise, anything I do to you, I do to me."*

A primary reason why this is an important core value is that from time-to time every member of the team, group or family will make a mistake. When a mistake is made, in a group with high tolerance, the questions are: "What happened? "How do we fix it?" "How do we prevent it in the future?" "What did we learn from it?" The mistake is a blessing in disguise if we learn from it and correct it, rather than find fault.

HONESTY

We live in a society where lying is commonplace and condoned. In our busy lives we often forget the simple truths that can carry us through tumultuous times. Such ancient truths as: *Oh, what a tangled web we weave when first we practice to deceive.* It is important for us to realize this little ditty is indeed a truism. Sometimes truth is painful, but we need to know truth never encumbers us nor entraps us.

The spiritual teacher, Emmett Fox, has defined wisdom as the perfect blending of honesty and love. Honesty or truth without love can be very cruel. Love without intelligence can be just as destructive. Honesty, even if painful, when blended with compassion is not of itself destructive and can strengthen the bonds of love and trust.

AND NOW THE KEYSTONE VALUE

NURTURE or NURTURING—A PRIMARY VALUE of CARING PEOPLE

Nurture: *Anything that nourishes.* American Heritage Dictionary

People with this value are genuinely concerned about the welfare and well-being of others. It is the "keystone" value that binds the other core values together. Nurturing implies that one also has empathy. Two psychologists at the University of Nebraska, Doctors Bill Hall and Don Clifton, after years of research, concluded that empathy cannot be taught—if we have it we were born with it.

DR. STEPHEN COVEY'S GREAT CONTRIBUTIONS:

NOTE: One of the greatest contributions of the recently departed Harvard professor, Dr. Covey, to our society was his book *The Seven Habits of Highly Successful People*. The following essay is without doubt equally true and useful.

THE ONE THING THAT CHANGES EVERYTHING

There is one thing that is common to every individual, relationship, team, family, organization, nation, economy, and civilization throughout the world—one thing which, if removed, will destroy the most powerful government, the most successful business, the most thriving economy, the most influential leadership, the greatest friendship, the strongest character, and the deepest love.

On the other hand, if developed and leveraged, that one thing has the potential to create unparalleled success and prosperity in every dimension of life. Yet, it is the least understood, most neglected, and most underestimated possibility of our time.

That one thing is trust.

Trust impacts us 24/7, 365 days a year. It undergirds and affects the quality of every relationship, every work project, every business venture, and every effort in which we are engaged. It changes the quality of every present moment and alters the trajectory on outcome of every future moment of our lives—both personally and professionally.

Contrary to what most people believe, trust is not some soft, illusive quality that you either have or you don't; rather trust is a pragmatic, tangible, actionable asset that you can create—much faster than you probably think possible.

While corporate scandals, terrorist threats, office politics, and broken relationships have created low trust on almost every front, I contend that the possi-

bility to establish, grow, extend, and restore trust is not only vital to our personal and interpersonal well-being; it is the key leadership competency of the new global economy.

I am also convinced that in every situation, nothing is as fast as the speed of trust. And, contrary to popular belief, trust is something you can do something about. In fact, you can get good at it!

PARTNERSHIPS

Let us consider the possibility that every relationship, at some level, is a partnership. The failure rate of partnerships is undeniably high. It is my contention and observation that if high trust exists in the partnership, be it personal, professional or business, it cannot fail. Please consider that high trust can result in the dissolution of a partnership, marriage or other, which may be in the best interest of all concerned and therefore is not a failure.

The Problem

If there is an adequate, open and honest "courtship" preceding the formation of the partnership; be it marriage, business, or friendship, the partners will be clear on the *expectations* of each other. However, without exception, those expectations will change over time. If the partners can openly and honestly discuss their differences, including changed expectations, it will be because of the trust in their relationship. One of the great benefits of high trust is that it enables the participants to make decisions quickly that are in the best interest of all concerned. This most valuable condition can exist when all players have no secrets from one another—their "cards face up."

There is, in my opinion, one prerequisite for high trust to develop. That requirement is shared core values, as stated above. Most people share these values. It is better to assume that your associates share these values with you unless they give you reason to think otherwise.

INTELLECTUAL HONESTY

We've all heard the term many times. But what does it really mean? I checked a couple of reference books including exploring the subject on the internet. This concept was sacred to the writers of the ancient Jewish Torah. Reading about this subject from several sources has led me to believe intellectual honesty means being honest with one's self—nothing more—nothing less. But let's explore it a bit.

In recent years we have also heard the term "in the box." My "senior citizen" (read *old-fashioned*) understanding of that term is that if I am "in the box" I will have greatly increased difficulty being effective in my communications and therefore have greater difficulty accomplishing my objectives. Additionally, if I am in the box I am less likely to be a team player. Not a good place to be.

I can put myself in the box by doing something that might be greatly, or even marginally, in violation of my value system and trying to justify it. That means making excuses—often inside my own head—rationalizing. Putting me in the box begins with self-betrayal. *Self-betrayal,* by definition is: *A failure to act on what I feel compelled to do for another. Or, failing to do what my intuition tells me is the right thing!* For example it might be something as commonplace and mundane as not helping other team members or family members clean the room at the end of a difficult day, when my guts tell me I should; or empty the dish washer, even though I did it last time—or any other avoidance of an action that would be kind and in the interest of others. And, therefore in my best interest! **Self-betrayal is violating my feelings.**

The real problem is what happens next. My avoidance of responsible behavior leads to feelings of guilt, which in turn leads to rationalizing and blaming others. The consequence of this is *self-deception.* Said another way it is intellectual dishonesty. To salve my conscience, my ego will lead me to blame others and I become the victim. At the conscious level I can rationalize this and be successful at avoiding responsibility and perhaps blaming others. ***But at a deeper level avoidance of responsibility leads to the penalty of reduced self-worth and a sense of powerlessness greatly reducing my quality of life.***

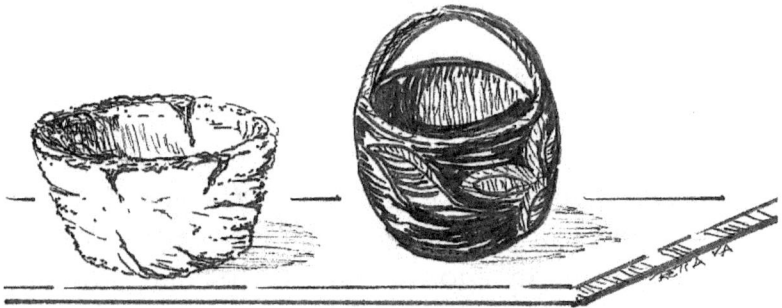

ACCEPTING RESPONSIBILITY FOR OUR HISTORY AND OUR FUTURE WORKS

MORE ON THE FIRST GREAT TRUTH—
You Will Become What You Think

PERHAPS THE GREATEST or at least one of the greatest books ever written about this subject is *As a Man Thinketh*. It was written by English author and poet James Allen in the first decade of the 20th century. The late Earl Nightingale, highly respected American author, philosopher and teacher, suggested that Allen realized he had written a masterpiece and in the interest of maximum distribution chose not to copyright the book—any publisher could print it and sell it. The efficacy of that decision is that it is readily available in book stores today and it is likely that the only book to outsell it in the last 100 years is the Bible. The beauty and wisdom of Allen's thinking is readily apparent and can even be experienced if we thoughtfully consider the following;

EXCERPTS FROM: *AS A MAN THINKETH*

• YOUR TRUE SELF REVEALED

A man does not come to poverty or go to jail through the tyranny of fate or circumstances, but by the pathway of base thoughts and desires. Nor does a pure minded man suddenly fall into crime by stress of external force. The criminal thought has long been secretly fostered in his heart, and the hour of his sin revealed its gathered power. Circumstance does not make the man; it reveals him to himself. No such conditions can exist in a man as vice and its attendant sufferings apart from viscous inclinations, or virtue and its pure happiness without the continued cultivation of virtuous aspirations.

• A MASTER OF FORCES

. . . And you, too, will realize the vision (not the idle wish) of your heart, be it base or beautiful, or a mixture of the two, for you will always gravitate toward that which you most love. In your hands will be placed the exact results of your own thoughts; you will receive what you earn; no more, no less. Whatever your present environment may be, you will fall, remain, or rise with your thoughts, your vision, and your ideal. You will become as small as your controlling desire; as great as your dominant aspiration.

• LUCK IS A MISNOMER

The thoughtless, the ignorant, and the indolent, seeing only the apparent effects of things and not the things themselves, talk of luck, of fortune, and chance. Seeing a man grow rich they say, "How lucky he is!" Observing another become intellectual, they exclaim, "How highly favored he is!" And noting the saintly character and wide influence of another, they remark, "How chance aids him at every turn!" They do not see the trials and failures and struggles . . . They do not know the darkness and the heartaches; they see only the light and the joy, and call it "luck."

MORE ON THE SECOND GREAT TRUTH—
Whatever You Want, Give It Away

Any treatise on giving would be incomplete without thoroughly exploring giving's counterpart—receiving. In our culture it is commonplace for many generous, giving people to have emotional difficulty accepting a gift. Some years ago I was introduced to the idea that giving and receiving is the same thing. This idea is advanced in *A Course in Miracles*. The following personal experience may bring that concept into greater focus:

Some psychologists have strange and perhaps uncomplimentary things to say about people who collect things. In spite of those so-called learned opinions most of us are, or have been, collectors of something.

In my youth I had a collection of rifle ammunition and another of mineral samples. Later I collected antique bottles I dug from refuse dumps of Colorado ghost towns. Perhaps my most interesting collection (and the only one of which I have some remnants) was of Native American artifacts.

I have added little to this collection in recent years. However, I frequently think of one major lesson this hobby brought to me.

In the 1960s I was conducting management training classes for Mountain Bell Telephone in El Paso, Texas on a regular basis. Each trip was two weeks long. I usually spent the interim weekend pursuing my hobby of collecting artifacts in rural areas.

After I became friends with some of the locals who participated in the training classes, they invited me to go with them on a weekend expedition into Mexico. The organizers of the outing were after some good old R and R—in this case "raucous rowdyism." But for me it was an opportunity to hunt artifacts in an area rich in Indian history.

I found and was able to bring home several beautiful pieces—stone ax heads and matate and mono stones (used to grind grain). But I failed to find a prized *olla* (pronounced oh-ya), or bowl, for which these Indians were noted.

When we returned to El Paso one Sunday evening, one of my hosts invited me to view his collection of artifacts. He escorted me to his game room. There before me on two shelves were several of the most magnificent ollas I had ever seen along with some very plain and drab ones. I picked up and admired a fine dark one that had a beautiful patina and was intricately carved. After I put it back on the shelf and examined the others, including the drab ones, my friend said, "Bud, I would like you to pick one you would really like to have."

He knew as well as I which one I liked. His smiling face, eyes twinkling with expected pleasure, fell when I selected one of the colorless, drab bowls. I realized instantly what I had done. But it was too late. I had denied my friend the joy of giving me a cherished gift.

Who Is the Giver?

Who is the giver, he who can divest?
Or he who is receiving
with thanks he can express?

I won't complain about the past,
the future I don't know.
But just today I think I see forever in the glow.
The chance for us to learn and grow
is always opportune.
Tomorrow is just a breath away
and is yesterday so soon.

But time we have in like amount,
each one the stated moment,
For each of us a different route,
along life's path intent.
We stress ourselves and waste and fret
and miss the beauty known,
And rush right past the quiet part
and wonder what went wrong.

But time there is to do our task
and love the life we're living.
We have enough and will complete
if we can learn of giving.

We need the wind, we need the snow,
we need the cold and rain.
There is something else we need to know
GIVING AND RECEIVING ARE THE SAME

Who is the giver, she who can divest?
Or she who is receiving
with thanks she can express?

MORE ON THE THIRD GREAT TRUTH—
You Are In Charge of Your Own Destiny

Internals and Externals

There is a label behaviorists assign to those who accept responsibility for their past thinking and behavior and accept that they have created their present reality; they are referred to as "Internals." Their counterparts in life, who disagree with this philosophy, are referred to as "Externals." Externals believe in *fate, luck* and *powerful others.* [From Dr. J.B Rotter's book, *Locus of Control,* a book I strongly recommend]

Before we explore the characteristics of Externals and Internals let us review a concept that greatly influences how people think, and as we have previously reviewed, **what we think determines what we become.**

ANOTHER LOOK AT LOVE AND FEAR

There is a concept, still relatively little known (except for students of *A Course in Miracles*) that there are only two basic human emotions; love and fear. All other emotions are derivatives of one or the other. For a few examples: jealousy; greed; vengeance; selfishness and anger are derivative emotions of fear.

Conversely, tolerance; generosity; compassion; and happiness are all derivatives of love.

Further, it is important to understand that fear and love are opposites and co-variables. We know they are opposites because we cannot be loving and fearful at the same time. They are co-variables because if fear goes up in our lives, love goes down and vice-versa.

All healthy people want to be happy. The happiest people we know live with less fear. Is this "fate and luck" or do they have a measure of control over their state of being? If we can accept this concept, it follows that since we want to be happy we want to live with less fear—a no brainer! But how can we possibly control that?

All of us have experienced events, over which we thought we had no control that created great fear in our lives and perhaps its derivatives of sadness, anger or revenge. ***Let us agree not to spend our precious energy on things over which we have no control! A quick and short analysis will prove to us however that the vast majority of events bringing unhappiness into our lives <u>are under our control!!</u> There is a very large and growing contingent of people who accept that there are no accidents.*** It is here we want to take charge and create more of the future we want. **How do we do that?**

Who is An Internal?

Perhaps first and foremost an Internal is an optimist. Optimists have positive expectations for the future. Secondly, Internals have a trusting nature. This is not to suggest that they are gullible or naïve. Rather, they tend to easily accept the findings of psychologist Dr. J.B. Rotter, who concluded the following after several major investigations: ***"It is better to trust unless you have reason not to."*** Findings supporting this statement include:

✧ Trusters are happier people.

✧ Trusters have more friends than non-trusters.

✧ Trusters are healthier and live longer than non-trusters.

✧ "Internals" have higher trust levels than "externals."

✧ There is no correlation between trust level and level of intelligence.

✧ Non-trusters have higher heart attack rates.

✧ Low trusters are more likely to lie and cheat. Researchers found that even in a game which allowed cheating high trusters didn't cheat.

✧ People who cheat are more frequently cheated.

✧ Trusters are more punitive to dishonest persons.

✧ You can't be defensive and trusting at the same time.

✧ Trust requires giving up some measure of control.

✧ People who do not trust are less trustworthy.

First Prerequisite to Become an Internal

The first prerequisite to achieve greater quality of life—more happiness—is that you give up the commonly held belief that to be happy, prosperous, successful and healthy is complicated! **It is not, it is deceptively simple!** It is also recommend that you guard against another commonly held belief; "if it is simple it is easy." That is not always true, it can be very difficult, but you can do it! It is easy for most people to accept that our quality of life is governed to a very great extent by our decision making.

The spiritual study, *A Course in Miracles* teaches that the only place we have any control on our lives is our thoughts. Philosophers have told us for centuries that, "The thought is father of the deed!" Once we have accepted—"own"—a thought, be it beautiful or ugly—continued entertainment of it will eventually cause our behavior to bring it to reality. If you change what you think, you change your behavior and you change your life!

The Second Prerequisite to Become an Internal

It is necessary for growth oriented persons to overcome another barrier to their happiness. That barrier is overcome by accepting that with effort and discipline we can control our thinking. Yes, every one of us has negative, ugly, mean-spirited, even vicious thoughts from time to time. Often we have no idea where they came from. ***But we do become what we think, and we want to be happy.*** If we are sad, depressed, angry or mean-spirited in any way we are not happy!

Firstly, know that to entertain any negative, fear-based, or angry thought is a choice. We have the ability to exercise the discipline to reject that thought and replace it with one that will help us achieve our goal of being happy. It is imperative, for this concept to be useful, that we discipline ourselves to remember as previously suggested, and ACIM teaches, *"I can choose again."*

The Role of the Subconscious Mind

Quite possibly one of Dr. Sigmund Freud's greatest contributions to our current understanding of human nature is that humans have a sub-conscious mind—a memory repository where all that we have seen, felt, thought, read, and/or experienced is stored. It is likewise accepted that our sub-conscious mind influences our behavior. Hypnotic regression has demonstrated that everything we have experienced is still part of our memory banks. An apt analogy is to think of our subconscious mind as a pool without a drain—we can only put information in—we can take nothing out!

The Public Media and Negativity

Pessimism and negative attitudes are pandemic in our society, greatly influencing our subconscious. Newspapers, radio and television news broadcasts are heavily dominated by the ugly, vile things that human beings do to each other. It seems that to be newsworthy even the weather must be horrible! This ugliness has a decidedly negative effect on the psyche of most of the thoughtful people in our society. Be aware that everything that we read, hear and see becomes part of our subconscious pool!

Unless we are willing to consciously work on the "ph" of our subconscious pool it becomes heavily contaminated with negative information that does not serve our happiness objective!

Those who claim to know something about changing our behavior, which we know requires changing our thinking, tell us, "Unless we change the input we will not change the output." So, what do we change? A starting place is to commit to wean ourselves from the addiction to the broadcast media. Most of us want to be responsible citizens and to fulfill that commitment we must be informed.

An experiment that can lead us to a reduced level of negativity and still help us be adequately informed is to avoid broadcast media, T.V. and radio, for a period of time. For at least two or three weeks commit to getting our news from a newspaper or on-line through the internet—not because it is less negative, but because we can **edit** it. During this time we will read only those articles that we want to know about or think we need to know about. There is no need for us to load our subconscious pools with the ugly details about a mother that murdered her babies or other equally horrendous stories.

Further, to adequately assess the impact of this period, it is important that we listen to harmonious, uplifting music, and make it a daily habit to read something about the nobler side of human behavior. We can do this through reading poetry or perhaps a daily spiritual message that puts kindness, beauty and positive thoughts into our subconscious pool and reduces the negative "ph."

The Third Prerequisite to Improved Life—Changing Decision Making

If you choose to experience the affect of a period of time of reduced negative input (limiting your exposure to broadcast media) you can maximize the benefit of the experiment by adding another activity—**commit to *attempting* to make only love-based decisions during this period.** Many, perhaps most, of the decisions we make every day have no emotional component, for example, do I wear the green shirt or the blue one today? Yet, the decisions that do have an emotional component have the greatest impact on the quality of our relationships and therefore on the quality of our lives.

Please consider this; *you never make a decision with an emotional component by yourself—you make it in* **collaboration** *with your fear side or your love side—the fear side is your ego—the love side is the Holy Spirit.*

The following parable can help us clarify the simplicity of choosing our own future.

The great teacher/healer/humanitarian, Elizabeth Kubler-Ross told us that each of us has within himself/herself a Mother Teresa and a Hitler!

Testing the Concept

To test this concept is very simple and will require no more than a few minutes each morning for a few weeks. During the early part of each day make a short list of four or five things which, if they happened that day, would contribute to an ideal day for you. Date the list and put it in a drawer. Next, make

THE INDIAN GRANDPA PARABLE

An old American Indian was teaching his grandson about life. "A fight is going on inside me, you, and every human," he said to the boy. "It is a terrible fight and it is between two wolves. One is evil—he is anger, hatred, envy, sorrow, regret, greed, arrogance, self-pity, guilt, resentment, inferiority, lies, false pride, superiority and ego. The other wolf is good—he is joy, peace, love for others, self love, hope, serenity, humility, kindness, benevolence, empathy, generosity, truth, compassion, and faith."

The grandson thought about his grandfather's words and then asked, "Which wolf will win?"

The old Indian replied simply, "The one you feed."

the commitment that to the best of your ability that day you will strive to make love-based decisions on every decision that has an emotional component.

Only rarely will you be confused about whether a decision is love-based or fear-based. If you are a follower of the teachings of Jesus—and you need not be a Christian if only you accept that his commitment was to teach love—you only need to ask, "What would Jesus do?" After giving the process a fair trial, at least a two or three weeks, review your dated lists and determine if you had more ideal (happy) days.

MORE OF WHAT WORKS

Contributions of Deepak Chopra

Dr. Deepak Chopra is highly regarded around the world as a physician of Western and Ayurvedic medicine, a philosopher and a spiritual leader. I highly recommend his books. Three of my favorites are *The Seven Spiritual Laws for Success; How to Know God* and *The Third Jesus.*

In the *Seven Spiritual Laws* book, law number two is The Law of Giving and Receiving. His very convincing analogy compares the flow of money to the flow of blood—if the outflow stops, it coagulates and blocks the inflow channel. To restore the flow in the receiving channel we only need to unblock the outflow through the "giving channel."

In addition to *The Course in Miracles* teaching that giving and receiving are the same is the teaching that *"the only way to keep anything is to give it away."* It parallels Jesus' teaching of "cast your bread on the water and it will be returned to you multiplied."

When I was a small boy attending Sunday school
at the First Baptist Church in Florence, Colorado I
thought Jesus was only referring to putting "good-
ness" on the water. I have since come to realize that
"this knife cuts both ways!" Putting meanness on
the water is also returned multiplied and in kind.

It occurs to me that all of the natural laws "that
work" are very simple:

✧ Whatever I do for you, I do for me.

✧ Whatever I do to you, I do to me.

✧ I cannot gain from another's loss.

✧ I cannot lose from another's gain.

✧ If I have something I cannot give away, I don't
own it, it owns me.

✧ Truth sets you free.

✧ The more I accumulate, the more I have to look
after, is that owning or being owned?

[NOTE: The above way of thinking has been greatly influenced by two books: *The Way of the Wolf*
by Malcom Bell and from *The Tao of Leadership*
by Erich Heider]

Based on my observations, and my personal
experience, giving freely is initially a very difficult
and life influencing behavior to master. Through the
years I have known many kind, loving people who
have not mastered the art of giving—if indeed it is
an art. The question can be asked, perhaps must be
asked, "Do we trust Jesus teaching?" If I give you my
love it is easy to trust that I still have it. But what if
I give you some of my money? What happens to our

emotional thought processes now? Another question
we should ask is, "Did I give with reasonable pru-
dence?" For example, if we give our children too
much money we run the risk of destroying their
motivation to provide for themselves.

**The bottom line reality is that I don't—I can-
not—own anything! This includes real estate,
jewelry, stocks and bonds, material objects,
family members or friends. Nothing! These are
"callable loans" which will be called and can be
called or cancelled at any time.**

Every human being leaves this life with the same
amount of material accumulations we came with —
none! Could it be that to give away our wealth before
we leave is a better way to go? If we believe in an
afterlife do we take anything with us? None of us
know for certain but perhaps the answer is, ***"Yes,
we take with us any love-based actions that
enriched the loving nature of our souls!"***

A few years ago I was the guest lecturer at a
District Dental Society meeting in Cincinnati, Ohio.
My host, with whom I had the opportunity to become
quite well acquainted, was a red-haired, Irish Catholic
dentist, about 45 years old. Near the end of my visit
he told me the following story:

> *"About five years ago my son Billy had a
> serious asthma attack and had to be rushed
> to a hospital for life saving, emergency care.
> He had had many similar attacks that began
> when he was an infant. The day after his last
> attack I received a call from Billy's doctor
> asking me to come to his office for a visit.*

When I arrived the physician described the seriousness of Billy's illness and suggested that unless we took more aggressive action we were in danger of losing him during some future attack. He said the only solution he knew of was for Billy to become a live-in patient at the National Jewish Hospital in Denver, Colorado. He explained he would need to be there from nine months to a year.

I was actually sobbing as I tearfully told the physician that my wife and I were almost forced into bankruptcy because of Bill's medical expenses and we had no money. He asked me to bring my wife and come back to his office the next afternoon. When we arrived we were introduced to an elderly man who sat quietly off to the side as the doctor again reviewed his recommendations for our son. I again told him, we, too, wanted that for Billy but that we had no way of paying for it. The elderly gentleman interrupted the conversation and said, 'You don't have to have the money, I have it.'

"Billy spent the next nine months at National Jewish. That was over five years ago. Our son has not had a serious problem since. During the time he was in Denver, every four weeks, two round-trip airline tickets were mailed to our house. Our benefactor made it very clear there was only one way we could repay him— someday help someone else."

The elderly man in the above story was Jewish. Jews have a well deserved reputation for being committed to what is commonly referred as charity or philanthropy. During November 2007, which is National Philanthropy Month, I had the good fortune to read about it, from the Jewish perspective, in the now defunct *Rocky Mountain News*. The article was written by Doug Sesserman, CEO of the Allied Jewish Federation, a philanthropic organization. Sesserman explained that the word most commonly used in Judaism to describe this is *tzedakah*. The word means "righteousness" and is derived from the Hebrew word *tzedek* which means "justice." In his article he says, *"Whenever we give of ourselves to the greater good, we, in our own small way, are bringing justice to the world."*

He went on to explain that the 12th Century Jewish sage, Moses Maimonides defined the eight levels of *tzedakah*. The Sage believed that the act must be fulfilled in a way that preserved the dignity of the recipient of the deed and he created the following hierarchy:

1. The donor gives unwillingly, but, nevertheless gives.
2. The donor gives cheerfully but not enough.
3. The donor gives enough but not until he is asked.
4. The donor gives before being asked.
5. The recipient knows the identity of the donor, but the donor does not know the identity of the recipient.

6. The donor knows the identity of the recipient, but the recipient does not know the identity of the donor.

7. Neither the recipient nor the donor knows the identity of the other.

8. The donor helps the recipient help himself or herself by extending a loan, joining in a partnership, or providing training that will give the recipient a "hand up" rather than a "hand out." This is the highest form of *tzedakah*.

Mr. Sesserman asks us to examine, *"On which rung of Maimonides ladder do we stand—are we giving willingly, cheerfully, and sufficiently?*
Are we doing what is just by doing what is right? And, perhaps most importantly of all, are we doing our part to change the world."

Let's not leave this idea quite yet. What was the quality of life experienced by the prudent, generous giver? I do not know of any scientifically controlled investigations that could give us concrete information. Yet, I believe observations of happy people, who are generous and prudent givers, attests to the cause and effect and the admonition from Jesus; **"Cast your bread on the waters and it will be returned to you multiplied."**

Chapter Four

A Beautiful Future for Humankind—A Growing Phenomenon

THROUGHOUT HISTORY there have been countless times when some prognosticator has predicted the end of the world—Armageddon. Often the person making such a prediction is a religious zealot and tells the world it is man's sinfulness that is bringing about this horrendous end—perhaps another attempt to control by fear! There have also been many prognosticators who have predicted the coming of what some call The Age of Aquarius—a time of world peace, tolerance and love.

Many spiritual leaders today have openly predicted a major shift or transformation/transition of human thought and culture in a positive direction in the near future. Some of these supporters of the predicted shift to more peace and prosperity have been influenced by the Mayan Calendar which ended 21 December 2012. Some suggested that the coming of that date would be Armageddon.

A best-selling book in the late 1970's was
The Aquarian Conspiracy by Marilyn Ferguson.
The author advanced the idea that there exists a large
and unorganized but very influential group of people
who are intent on doing good things for humankind
without making a lot of noise about it or taking credit.

Frequently these "positive prognosticators" reference the concept of "critical mass." The concept is
that when the numbers of minds that are focused on
love-based, positive expectations reach critical mass,
wave after wave of people will experience an
unplanned transformation in their thinking. Peace,
harmony, tolerance and love will become the norm
rather than the opposite conditions brought about by
dwelling on fear. Please consider the following essay:

The Wave of the Future

Wise men have told us for centuries that the only
constant in our world is change. Some of these
same philosophers have said that the great majority of people fear change—quite to the contrary—
many people welcome it with open minds and
positive expectations. It is also true that the vast
majority of people today live with varying but
almost constant levels of fear on a daily basis.
There is a plethora of information in *A Course in
Miracles* and *The Way of Mastery* and other writ-
ings that helps spiritual seekers accept that fear
does not enable us, rather it is an unnecessary and
debilitating emotion that weakens us. The hearts
and minds of those students who have already
been exposed to love-based thinking, as opposed
to fear-based thinking, know it is a choice. Many

are making the choice to reject fear! It is predicted that one day, in the near future, a critical mass of love-based thinkers will be reached and that people all over the planet Earth will come down with love-based thinking in epidemic proportions. This will greatly reduce the current and more common fear-based decision making prevalent in our world today—the agenda of fear-based people is *"What's in it for me?" Many may find themselves inexplicably thinking, "What's in the best interest of all people, including me?"* They may be unaware of the transition in their thinking that has changed from "agenda" to "mission."

AN ESSAY ON "RIGHT THINKING"

Motivation research has demonstrated that, for most people, while knowing that money is important, also know it is not a primary motivator. So, why do people work? The simplest answer, and perhaps the best, is that people work to satisfy their *needs, wants,* and *desires.* Let's consider these one at a time:

- ✧ Needs—necessary for survival
- ✧ Wants—not necessary for survival but in the same category
- ✧ Desires—Includes things money cannot buy

Now let us ask, *What will motivate people who are not dissatisfied with what they have to greater levels of productivity?* The answer is: Any event that increases feelings of self-worth and confidence. We want things that money can buy but we also *desire* things money cannot buy. To take this thought process to its next higher level let us now consider being *agenda driven* and it's near opposite, *mission driven.*

Agenda Driven

In our culture we are taught from an early age that to be a winner is highly desirable and that winners are strongly goal oriented people. When we clarify our goals we have identified predetermined outcomes that we want, be they needs, wants or desires. When we have an agenda it is usually designed to satisfy **our** needs, wants, and/or desires—sometimes to the disadvantage of others. What will serve us better?

Mission Driven

When we are agenda driven, and motivated to achieve our predetermined outcome, we are concerned with, *What's in it for me?* When we are responding to our nobler emotions—our mission— our genuine concern is, ***How can I serve?***

It has been scientifically demonstrated that positive thoughts have positive energy and this energy creates an emotional environment affecting all people who are in that field of energy, as the following story demonstrates:

> Not long ago I was conducting a sales and team building seminar for a group of real estate sales people in Bangor, Maine. When I introduced the concept of being Mission Driven as a sales technique several sales people made comments to the effect that being mission driven couldn't work in real estate—a comment from a real estate salesman was, *"It wouldn't work in real estate. Real estate*

is to cutthroat." When it appeared that the last of the opposition to the concept had been voiced an attractive, gray-haired, grandmotherly lady stood up and said, *"I've never referred to it as being mission driven but that has been my sales technique for the past several years. I came to adopt this style quite by accident. One month I had the good fortune to exceed my monthly sales goal in the first week. For the rest of that month, with each potential client, I concentrated on "how can I help this person?" I had never experienced such appreciation and acceptance as I did for the remainder of that month and I have never deviated from that approach since."* **The sixty-five year old woman had been the top sales person in the agency for three consecutive years!**

The Wave of the Future:

NOTE: The following was influenced by *Symptoms of Inner Peace.* Written by author Saskia Davis, 1984.

Some indications that one is under the influence of a positive world future:

✧ An acceptance that I shall experience more love, peace and happiness in my life if I make more love-based decisions.

✧ A tendency to think and act spontaneously, influenced by feelings of what is right, rather than on fears based on past experiences.

✧ Accepting that happiness is a decision and if I make a decision that will bring unhappiness I can choose again! (A major teaching of *A Course in Miracles.*)

✧ Accepting that I am not capable of judging other people, their behavior or events. (I can never have all of
the facts and I cannot know what happens next.)

✧ I cannot know what another truly needs, therefore, for me to give correction in inappropriate.
Yet, I have a moral obligation to share any
wisdom I may have with anyone who wants it.

✧ A loss of the ability to worry. (*Stop Worrying and
Start Living or utilize a proven exercise included
at the end of this chapter.*)

✧ A loss of interest in conflict, pain, horror and
violence as entertainment.

✧ Frequent, overwhelming episodes of appreciation—
accepting joy-based tearfulness.

✧ Develop the concept of *"ALLOWING."* An increasing tendency to accept things as they happen—
It is as it is—(credit to Ekhart Tolle) rather than
wanting and trying to make them happen "my
way." This includes behavior and actions of others
of which I do not approve.

✧ An increased ability to accept, with appreciation,
the love and gifts given to me by others as well as
the uncontrollable urge for me to extend love and
gifts to others.

✧ An abhorrence of racial, ethnic, religious, gender
or life style jokes.

✧ A greater desire to be happy than right.
(Another teaching of ACIM)

✧ An increased tendency to collaborate and
cooperate, instead of competing.

ELIMINATING THE GREATEST BARRIER TO PERSONAL PEACE—WORRY

THE WORRY EXERCISE

Worry is more common than the common cold. But unlike the common cold there is a cure for worry!

There is a little known, yet easily understood concept that, when accepted, removes this barrier. As previously mentioned in this writing students of *A Course in Miracles* have been introduced to this concept through studying the *Course*. The concept is so simple that, when understood and accepted, one might marvel at the lack of general awareness.

At the risk of being redundant let's review this important information one more time. ***There are only two basic human emotions, LOVE and FEAR.*** Labeled emotions, such as jealousy, revenge, anger, greed, selfishness, prejudice, self-pity, superiority, control, etc., are obviously fear-based. Love-based emotions include: generosity, tolerance, compassion, acceptance, freedom and equality.

The determining factor on reducing or eliminating fear/worry is ***the emotional component of the decisions we make!*** If we make more love-based decisions we live with more love in our lives. Therefore we enjoy more happiness and the other positive, emotionally-based states. Conversely, if we make more fear-based decisions we live with the emotionally-based states that fear creates, such as: anger, revenge, selfishness, helplessness, etc. It is also important to understand that worry is fear— *fear of the future.* Ekhart Tolle and other teacher/philosophers have helped us know that the future does not exist—there is only now.

Another great teacher, helping us to overcome worry, also previously mentioned, was the late Dale Carnegie. His book *How to Stop Worrying and Start Living* has helped millions become unhooked from the addiction of worry.

[One of the major turning points in my life was taking the Dale Carnegie Human Relations Course when I was 27 years old.]

The following exercise is designed to help anyone who chooses to **stop worrying.** It was greatly influenced by Dale Carnegie's book on that subject.

Contrary to the opinions of many psycho-therapists, ACIM teaches us that fear (worry) is a totally unnecessary human emotion and never solves problems. *It was love energy that enabled the small woman to lift the car that was crushing her husband!* Love enables us—fear immobilizes us.

GIVING UP WORRY

In Carnegie's book he suggests that people who worry had a "worry teacher," probably in the formative years of their youth. That was certainly true in my case. My Grandmother Ham gave me many, many beautiful thoughts and therefore values when I was a young boy—she also was the family worry teacher as the following story illustrates:

My grandparents lived on a small farm adjacent to the small farm of my family. There was about 50 yards between the houses. I was very common for Grandmother to come over to our house in the evenings after supper. Her favorite chair was next to the kitchen cook stove where she would enjoy a cup of coffee and conversation.

One evening in late fall she arrived looking harried or worried. My father noticed it and said, "Mother you look worried. What's wrong?"

She answered saying, "On my way over here this evening I took a little sashay through the wood yard and there is hardly any wood, just a few logs in the far corner. Then I looked in the coal house. There are just a few buckets of coal! If we get a big Blue Norther storm we will freeze in our beds!"

My father had been trained well! He was instantly worried. Then Grandmother continued; "Lonnie, I looked at the front tires of your old car—they are bald Lonnie. And the way you drive, you will be coming the corner at Ruger's store, hit that chuck hole, blow a front tire, hit the big ditch and be laying dead at the side of the road. And you with six little ones to feed!"

Now I was worried!

The Process

"Do not attack worry, attacking gives it validity, just release it, and let it be what it is—nothing."

The requirement for becoming worry free is to accept that the freedom which comes with being worry free is a desirable state. Said another way, you must want to give up worry! If you have been taught that as a responsible adult you have a duty to worry, you must first undo that teaching. The following exercise might help:

1 STEP ONE

"Who taught me to
worry?"_____

"How old was I when I was taught to
worry?"_____

Write a brief synopsis of a "worry lesson" you were
taught

_____
_____
_____
_____
_____
_____
_____
_____

Are you willing to become worry free? _____

Can you accept Jesus' teaching, *"All is well, have no
fear, I am with you?"*

**If you are ready and decide to give up worry,
it is now a matter of personal discipline. The
process is a simple one. The following exercise
has proven useful to millions of people. Quality
of life goes up when worry is reduced or elimi-
nated—yes it is possible! There is no better
investment of time and energy than the few
minutes this exercise requires every time worry
reduces your effectiveness.**

2 STEP TWO

Using a "Worry Log" (or any other paper that is handy), make a list of all the things that you are worried about right now.

WORRY LOG

DATE_____

_____
_____
_____
_____
_____
_____
_____
_____
_____
_____
_____
_____
_____
_____
_____
_____
_____
_____
_____
_____
_____
_____
_____
_____
_____

3 STEP THREE

Review each item on your list and work through it with the following process. Ask yourself:

'Other than pray, can I do anything about this?"

If your answer is "No", then draw a heavy, black line through the item and say it to yourself, aloud if possible.

> *"If I can't do anything about this except pray about it, I will pray,* **but I refuse to waste my energy and be unhappy about something over which I have no control."**

If your answer is "Yes," then ask yourself; "When?" If the answer is; "Now," then do it now! JUST DO IT! If the answer is, "Not until Monday, when I am back at work," then write a note to yourself and commit to taking care of the item Monday. Draw a heavy black line through the item and say**, "I refuse to reduce the quality of my weekend worrying about something I cannot change until Monday."**

FREQUENCY

It is impossible to say how frequently it would be useful for you to complete a "Worry Log" sheet and work through the process. The indication of the need is the pain, and/or nauseous feeling in the pit of the stomach. Nor can I tell you how long it will take before you consider yourself among the non-worriers of the world. But, I can give you information on a major clue, which can tell you whether you are on the right track or not.

Worry gives us that uncomfortable feeling in our solar plexus. It is indeed fear—fear of the future. Many people have lived with that discomfort for so long they may not remember what it is like not to have it. My experience in working with the process is this:

Frequently, after working through the process, carefully and thoroughly, I have experienced the absence of solar plexus pain—the creepy-crawley "gut ache"— within thirty minutes.

When you finally experience this you will know you are making progress. But even if you do not experience this after many sessions of completing the process, do not give up! **Remember, you have been a worrier for years—so hang in there.**

Should I join
real estate firm
or consulting
firm?

Chapter Five

A PREREQUISITE FOR GROWTH

I was reared in a fundamentalist Christian family of Southern Baptists. My highly respected Grandfather Ham was the spiritual/religious leader of the large family of aunts, uncles and cousins. Grandfather often delivered the Sunday sermon if the pastor was away. I enjoyed Sunday school and as a preschooler I was sure our Sunday school teacher, Mary Reece and Jesus' mother Mary, were one and the same. I answered "alter call" when I was eight years old and was soon baptized.

I usually sat with my grandfather and the other older men of the church in the "amen corner." I soon began adding my voice to theirs when the minister said something important and nodded in our direction. We would say in unison "Amen Brother!" When I started vocally participating my grandmother objected to my sitting with the elderly men but Grandfather said it was OK as long as I behaved myself.

I sat in the "Amen corner" and participated for a number of Sundays. One Sunday, when Grandfather was delivering the sermon, he said something that I thought was profound and paused to catch his breath. I thought that was the signal and I shouted out in my eight year old voice, Amen Brother! Of course, that was the last time I sat in the Amen corner!

It wasn't long after that I started hearing that I was supposed to be afraid of God. I found that difficult, if not impossible to accept, so I asked Grandpa about it. "Grandpa, if God loves me so much why do I have to be afraid of Him?" I remember his exact words to this very day: "Son, you don't have to be afraid of God, just be afraid of His wrath." That didn't make sense to me, then or ever.

We were taught that the souls of unrepentant sinners would spend eternity in the horrible torment of hell. And, it was never specified but there was at least one sin that was unforgivable!

The first Sunday of every month was communion Sunday and all who were baptized received a shot-glass of grape juice and a piece of cracker—the body and blood of Jesus. It was, for me a very solemn and meaningful event.

I distinctly remember praying on many communion Sundays, "God, if I am going to die this month please let it be by Tuesday or Wednesday." My thinking was that by mid-week I would have sinned and be going to hell and couldn't be redeemed until next communion Sunday!

It became obvious, in my immature thinking, that we had better follow the teachings of Jesus because of fear rather than just because it was the right thing to do! Sometime later, during my teen years, it became clear to my grandfather that I was rejecting fear-based, fundamentalist teaching. He then gave me, what I now believe was the best advice possible. He said, "Buddy, just remember to always ask God questions and keep an open mind." Not traditional Baptist teaching.

A Winding Spiritual Path—From Religion to Atheism

In my search for an acceptable doctrine and dogma I became a Methodist, later a Presbyterian and still later, after exploring Judaism, and the Roman Catholic beliefs, I became an Episcopalian.

The tipping point to me becoming an Anglican happened when I had a no win argument with a very popular Presbyterian minister about evolution. To my satisfaction I knew there had been a three-toed horse! A good friend, who had also been a Presbyterian, knew of the argument and suggested I check out being an Episcopalian.

While still part of the doctrine, the Anglicans didn't emphasize fear as strongly. The elderly priest who coached me resolved my other concern when he told me the Church didn't have a problem with evolution. After several years of being active as Vestryman, Junior Warden and Senior Warden, I eventually became a Lay Reader.

During this period of my life (in my late twenties) my young family and I lived in the small mountain town of Salida, Colorado. We had a delightful circle of young married couples and shared many events, especially playing the card game, Bridge, and dances and parties at the local Elks Club. During these years we shared many thoughts on philosophy and life.

This was in the late 1950s and two controversial books were discussed by several of our friends. One was *The Search for Brydie Murphy* by Morris Bernstein. The other was a biography of Edgar Casey, *Many Mansions* by Gina Cermanina. Both of these books strongly supported the belief of reincarnation. After initially rejecting reincarnation I read several books about Edgar Cayce and other literature supporting the concept. The concept of having many lives became an integral part of my studies and beliefs.

Several years later this line of thinking and studying led me to read a book titled *Great Religions by which Men Live*. This book is an objective, unbiased report on seven of the world's great religions.

After devouring the book I had to confront one of the greatest shocks of my life. I could no longer stand and recite the Nicene Creed, which is an integral part of the Episcopal worship service. In the Creed is the affirmation that Jesus is the only son of God.

Following a service, the priest, who was a good friend, asked, "Bud, are you ill?" I said, "No, but I would be lying to stand and recite the Creed." I became "a person of great interest" to the leaders of our congregation!

That idea that there was only one son of God had been ingrained into my thinking and belief system since I was a small boy. It became the "tipping point" that led to a rejection of all religious/spiritual, teaching and practice.

In a short period of time I professed atheism. The rejection of all religious dogma and doctrine and spiritual beliefs removed a heavy burden and I felt free. I quickly learned the arguments supporting atheism.

After several promotions in the management ranks of Mountain Bell Telephone, my family and I lived in Denver. It was here I become heavily involved with the Human Potential Movement, ala Drs. Abraham Maslow and Carl Rogers—a phenomenon of the 1960s. Four professors from Denver University and I formed a group to conduct personal growth retreats; largely referred to as "sensitivity training," "encounter groups" or "T" Groups. Spirituality was not part of the teaching.

Two of my new friends from DU were Jews and two were atheists. All four of them were PhDs. They are kind, generous and loving people of the highest integrity. Then and now I have strong love and the highest respect for them.

Another phenomenon of the time—late 1960s— was the formation of Denver Free University by a group of "hippy" college students. The "charter" of DFU was to provide learning opportunities for any one choosing to participate, as a teacher or student, in the widest variety of study topics. Including such topics as: writing poetry; witchcraft; physical conditioning; cooking; karate; sewing/knitting; wood carving; various kinds of art and painting, etc. I was asked to be the leader of Sensitivity Training. I conducted four groups. Each group of twelve people met one evening per week for fourteen weeks. I enjoyed working with these young people. I loved the hippies!

During one of the last sessions of the fourth group two young hippies said, "Bud, we think you would really enjoy this "far out" church that is different from anything you have ever experienced. Would you meet us there Sunday evening at 7:00 P. M.?" I agreed to do so.

The following Sunday evening I was at the church, The Temple of Harmony, a member of The Spiritualist Churches of America. Not surprisingly the hippies never showed up! The service was very different from any church I had ever visited. The group sang a few songs that were very different from any I had ever heard. The aged minister read the announcements for the week ahead and announced that in this church there were no sermons; we were there to learn and therefore we would receive a lecture. There were about 60 people in the congregation.

Following the lecture the minister asked several people in the congregation if they would "give him a hand."

Three people agreed and joined him on the speaker's platform, and sat on folding chairs. They began giving messages to people in the congregation and it soon became obvious that those on the platform were mediums or psychics. Each of them in turn identified a person in the congregation to receive a reading, such as, "I want to come to the lady in the black dress in the third row." The recipient responded with 'good evening' and the psychic would proceed: One message was: "I am in touch with a fatherly figure and he says I should tell you to have the brakes on your truck fixed before your next trip." Each psychic gave four or five readings.

The last to give readings was the elderly minister. After giving several readings to others he said, "I want to come to the young man in the back row in the leather jacket." I responded with the standard, "Good evening." He said, "I am in touch with a grandfatherly figure, he is a portly man with unusually thick, grey hair, thick glasses and bushy mustache and eyebrows.

He tells me to tell you to 'Make up your own gosh darn mind about religion,' that is what he says."

He described my grandfather perfectly, and included the words he would use. A few days later, after about a three year hiatus, I decided it was time for me to again explore spirituality. I became a regular at the Sunday evening service.

One Sunday evening as I was leaving the church the minister asked me if I would deliver the lecture the following Sunday evening. I readily agreed. I have no idea how he knew I was a public speaker. My lecture focused on the idea that life's problems were either mill-stones that could drown us or we could choose to learn from the problems and they would be stepping stones toward growth, peace and happiness. The message was well received and I became a frequent Sunday evening lecturer.

While attending the church, The Temple of Harmony, I received many useful readings. One of the most memorable occurred one Sunday evening when a visiting itinerant psychic visited the church. Upon entering the sanctuary each person was handed a short pencil and a 3"X5" card. When it became time for the psychic demonstration the congregation was instructed to write on the card the names of two people who had "crossed over"—their words for death—and a question we wanted to ask the psychic. I wrote the names of Joe Stovall, a Marine Corps buddy who was killed in Korea, and Grandpa Ham.

At the time I had decided to leave Mountain Bell Telephone Company after 20 years of employment. My title at the time was Organization Development Specialist. I was Mountain Bell's senior in-company management consultant.

I had two options for my next career. One was to become a real-estate salesman. I had a real-estate sales license and a friend who was a real estate broker. He assured me I would be successful very quickly. The other option was to join a friend who had a sales consulting firm. My sales consulting friend told me that many of his clients needed management consulting. My question for the psychic was, "Should I join the real-estate firm or the consulting firm?"

We were instructed to fold the cards to conceal the writing and they were collected. The visiting psychic was carefully and completely blind-folded and seated at a folding table in front of the congregation. The cards were deposited on the table in a large pile. He instructed the congregation to respond with "good evening" if we thought he was talking about our card. He did not unfold the cards. He would hold a card up, and just like Jonny Carson did on his show, and he would start talking about the card.

After delivering a number of readings he picked up a card and said, "I am in touch with two hams, wait, it is an old ham and a young ham, I also see a kitchen stove." I immediately responded with "good evening" and he said, "By all means join the consulting firm."

The Rest of the Story

I never used the real estate license. As of this writing I have been an independent consultant and life coach for more than 40 years! This event happened exactly as I have reported it! It is, for me, a ***"knowing"*** and dispels any doubt or thought that there might not be a "Greater Power."

MY INVOLVEMENT AS A MEDIUM OR PSYCHIC

The minister began asking me on a regular basis if I would "give him a hand" as a medium or psychic. I repeatedly said, "No." Until one Sunday evening, without hesitation or thinking about it, I said yes. I followed him and another regular participating psychic to the platform. I was panic stricken! Asking myself, "Why did I say yes? I have no idea about a reading."

When it was obvious it was my turn to give a reading I calmly said, "I want to come to the lady in the blue polka-dot dress in the third row." The black lady said the usual, "Good evening." I then said, "There is an older woman standing right beside you with her hand on your shoulder. She is wearing a red bandana, a red blouse and shawl and a full length blue denim skirt. She wants me to tell you she is very happy you are at this service."

The lady started to cry and thanked me for the message from her grandmother.

Then I said, "I will now come to the man in the blue suit in the back row." After the standard "good evening," I said, "Tomorrow you are planning to fire one of your employees. I am instructed to tell you to give him another chance."

Following the service the man in the blue suit came to me and said, "How did you know?" I told him I didn't have a clue. I had never seen the man before and haven't seen him since. That was the only time I gave readings from the platform.

Following the crossing over (passing) of the old minister I attended the services only sporadically and finally stopped my affiliation.

Many years later I conducted a two-day team-building meeting for a group of mental health workers. The meeting was held in a small ski resort in the off-season. Two young women accommodated our group by bringing our food and assisting in any way they could. After the meeting was over and I was preparing to leave I kept having the thought that I should tell one of the young women that she "should not settle for a taker." I had no way of knowing anything about the personal life of the young woman. I repeatedly rejected the thought but it continued with intensity. Finally I explained to her that I had an "intuition" to give her a message. She said, "Oh, please do." When I delivered the message she paled visibly, then hugged me and said, "Thank you, thank you, thank you!"

I am not certain it is "psychic," but many times as I have been delivering a lecture I have a feeling I am almost in a trance and the words I speak seem to come from outside of my conscious thought. They are invariably enthusiastically received.

Chapter Six

SOURCE MATERIAL FROM NEW THINKING

N *EW AGE SPIRITUALITY.* These three words raise fear-based reactions among many of my more conservative Christian friends. If you are one of those devoted people I solemnly request that you stick with me for a few more paragraphs. Please be assured that my request is not intended to influence you, in any way, to consider changing your religious and spiritual beliefs and practices. But it is intended to provide you information that might influence your level of tolerance of those who do accept this new thinking. As mentioned previously, I encourage experimentation.

"New Age"—What is it really?

Please consider the following questions:

✦ Do you agree Jesus taught only love?

✦ In the more than two-thousand years since his crucifixion do you believe we, as God's children, are satisfactorily practicing Jesus' teaching?

✦ Do you believe in miracles?

✦ Do you think our Creator stopped trying to educate His children with the writing of the Bible?

✦ Do you believe that heaven is reserved only for Christians?

✦ Do you accept Jesus' teaching, *"And greater things than these shall you do?"*

THE PHENOMENON OF "CHANNELED" MESSAGES AND BOOKS

CREATION of the BOOK *GOD CALLING*

In the early 1930's two elderly women met in London, England to discuss their poverty stricken, stress filled lives. One of the women remarked that one of Jesus' teachings was, *"Where two or more people meet in my name I am there also."* They began meeting on a daily basis and one of them received a message from Jesus each day. These channeled messages were then combined and printed in the book *God Calling*—a beautiful short message for each day of the year. The book is readily available in religious book stores today. It was edited by A. J. Russell

I was introduced to this book in 1988 by a dear friend who is a devoted, practicing Roman Catholic. With great sincerity he said, "Bud, God told me to give you this book." [He has been in my "inner circle" of friends for almost 40 years. He told me several years later that he almost didn't give me the book because of my possible reaction.] Indeed the book has been a God-send to me. I have been through it many, many times and have given it to many acquaintances. After drift-ing away from it several times I am again reading it daily.

It is indeed a New Age book. In this book, and all the other new age books I have read, there is not one reference to fearing God or His wrath! In the book *God Calling* there are many readings of Jesus saying, "Have no fear, I am with you."

In the 1970's another best selling, channeled book was *Seth Speaks*. Once again, there is no reference to fear being part of the teaching. If one cares to pursue this line of thinking there are many channeled books that support an all loving God, not a wrathful one.

Was It Necessary To Teach Fear?

I am comfortable in the knowing that God is now and always has been in charge of His creation—you, me and the entire universe. In the early centuries of Christianity the masses of the people were illiterate and very superstitious. **It is plausible that fear, and/or greater magic, was necessary for the teachings of Jesus to survive.**

I do not believe fear is necessary today. In every channeled book I have read (approximately 50) clearly the message is that God loves us unconditionally and offers us freedom (free will); forgiveness for mistakes; and wants us to have health, peace and prosperity. It is also taught that fear is a totally ego-based, unnecessary human emotion that weakens us.

The Creation of a New Age Course in Spiritual Learning—*A Course in Miracles*

During the late 1960's a very strange thing began to happen to Dr. Helen Schucman the co-chairperson of the Medical Psychology Department at Columbia University in New York City. She began having severe headaches and very disturbing dreams almost every night. She eventually discussed this with the department chairman, Dr. Bill Thetford. She told him that her major concern was that she might be losing her mind and experiencing a severe personality disorder. While experiencing these terrible headaches she had an overwhelming compulsion to write. He suggested that she try writing and see what happened. She reluctantly agreed to do so during the next painful episode.

The next day, after he typed up her short-hand writing, it was clear that Helen was being used as a "channel" by Jesus. This went on sporadically for the next seven years. This was an especially difficult time for her, in part because she was raised Jewish and professed atheism.

This writing continued into the 1970s. Eventually it was published as *A Course in Miracles*. This course has become the primary spiritual study for many millions of people all around the world. There is much more to this story and I encourage anyone interested to read one of many books detailing these very interesting events. One easy to read book, thoroughly explaining how ACIM came into being, is *Journey Without Distance,* by Robert Skutch.

Other Channeled Books

The previously mentioned books by former disc jockey, Neal Donald Walsch, *Conversations with God,* have positively influenced the peace and spiritual growth of millions of people world-wide. I am one, and I highly recommend them.

Perhaps there is a "fine line," or maybe no difference, between a writing that is "divinely inspired" and one channeled from the spirit world. This might include the previously quoted book, *As a Man Thinketh* by James Allen and the ever popular book, *The Prophet* by Kalil Gibran and also Rev. Norman Vincent Peale's book, *The Power of Positive Thinking,* and the text book that spawned *Alcoholics Anonymous.*

For several years one of the fastest growing religious groups in the world has been The Church of Latter Day Saints—Mormons. This religious group is definitely the result of a channeled book.

The *INTERVENTION* That Brought ACIM to the Author

My introduction to *A Course in Miracles* came in late summer, 1984 as described below. Please be assured the following is a totally factual account of my experience.

Beginning in 1981 and continuing through 1996 I was one of the founders and the first president of The Bob Barkley Foundation. The other founders were Dr. Robert Fraser of Austin, Texas and Dr. Donald Vollmer of Denver. In the 1970s Dr. Robert F. Barkley was one of the world's best known and most loved dentists. He was recognized interna-

tionally as the 'Father of Preventive Dentistry.' He lectured worldwide, even behind the "Iron Curtain," isolating Russia at the time. He was also my partner in a dental consulting company named Growth Services for Health Professionals. He was killed in a plane crash in August, 1977.

The foundation was formed to sponsor an annual gathering of dentist's and their families to extend Dr. Barkley's philosophy of quality patient care, learning and personal growth. We named the meeting The Rocky Mountain Rendezvous. The mission of the gathering soon became focused on providing opportunities for dentists, their staffs and families to improve family communications as well as to explore ways to better serve dental patients.

Without any conscious intent the meeting also began including the application of spiritual principles to our personal and professional lives. This transition was undoubtedly furthered by such spiritually oriented presenters as John Bradshaw, Dr. Bernie Segal, Dan Millman, Dr. Joan Borysinko, Dr. Larry Dossey, Dr. Rachel Naomi Remen, Dr. Emmitt Miller, Dr. Carl Hammerschlaug, Dr. Ashley Montague and others.

In the mid-1980's the meeting was attended by a gay dentist from Southern California. He was well known in his home state for conducting team building seminars for dental practices. He attended again the following year along with his partner.

At the conclusion of his second visit he approached me and proposed that he be one of the workshop presenters the following year. In my assessment of my interaction with him I am sure I was kind to him. But my fear based prejudices, of that time, made it impossible for me to welcome a homosexual as a presenter. **[Please note: I no longer entertain those prejudices.]**

A few months later UPS delivered a box containing three beautiful blue, hard bound books to my home. The three books were A Course in Miracles. *They were a gift from the gay dentist.*

Over the next few months I made several attempts to read the two larger books—The Text and The Workbook for Students. But they seemed much too religious—to "Christy" for me.

At that time I was also a member of a six man group—five business men and a college professor— we met once a month for an afternoon for the sole purpose of personal growth. The six of us held a personal growth retreat for a weekend a few months after I had received the ACIM *books. A short time later I received feedback from several of the members that I had been painfully critical and judgmental to one of our group members.*

I had received this feed-back many times in previous years—but this time I couldn't rationalize my way out of it. I accepted it as a barrier to my personal growth and committed, at a very meaningful level, to change and become more tolerant. I began earnestly seeking a "path" to help me achieve this change in behavior.

One afternoon I was riding my Schwinn exercise bike which was equipped with a reading stand. I had read a number of books while exercising. On this day I took one more stab at ACIM. This time I selected the smallest of the three books, The Manual for Teachers. *By the time I had read the first few pages I knew that this small book contained information that could help me with my commitment to become less judgmental. I have been a student of the Course ever since.*

About six years later, in 1992, I was the last of the featured speakers at the annual California State Dental Convention in Anaheim, California. At the conclusion of my presentation several dentists came forward to thank me for the lecture; the last one was the gay dentist. He said, "Bud, thank you, you did it again. Every time I listen to you or read your stuff it helps me."

I energetically responded to his remarks by saying, "Wait a minute. Please hear me when I tell you the books you sent me have greatly changed my life. I can never thank you enough!"

He responded by saying, "It was the strangest happening in my life. I was in a book store and saw the three volumes. Then I received a powerful intuitive message, I was told to buy the books and send them to you. I have never read them, nor do I know anyone else who has!

I shall be eternally grateful for the above reported Divine intervention in my life.

Following are a few of the life altering learnings I have gained, primarily from self-study, from ACIM:

✧ There is no order of difficulty in miracles.

✧ Miracles are natural.

✧ Miracles are teaching devices.

✧ There are no accidents. Everything we experience contains a lesson God would have us learn. If we chose to learn the lesson, which is part of every experience, even undesired experiences become precious gifts.

✧ Victimhood is always a choice. In truth there are no victims.

✧ Giving and receiving are the same.

✧ There are only two basic human emotions— love and fear.

✧ Fear invariably blocks my peace and happiness.

✧ When I have a mean-spirited, fear-based thought I can reject it and choose again! (Remember The Law of Attraction!)

✧ There is no death, only a transition when our spirit leaves the body.

✧ I am only required to have a "little willingness" to open my mind to new learning.

✧ There is no such thing as sin. We all make mistakes from which we can learn—when we learn from the mistake it becomes a gift!

✧ Let us be aware that when John Wycliffe translated the Vulgate Bible into the King James Version he translated the Latin word *peccatum* as sin. The correct translation is mistake or error!

Learning From *A Course in Miracles*

NOTE: Near the beginning of my self-study of ACIM I listened to a cassette tape recorded by Dr. Ken Wapnick. Dr. Wapnick has been the "guiding principal" of ACIM since its publication. One very important message from that tape, paraphrased a bit is: "If you come to something in the Course that you do not agree with or understand do not be concerned about it—keep right on studying."

NOTE: Dr. Wapnick was the founding principal of The Foundation for Inner Peace (publishers of *A Course in Miracles*) They can be contacted at P.O. Box 598 Mill Valley, California 94942. [Dr. Wapnick died in 2014]

ACIM was originally published in three separate volumes: The Text; Workbook for Students and Manual for Teachers. These have now been incorporated into one volume.

A learning that has been exceptionally useful for me is Lesson 98 in the Workbook for Students: ***I will accept my part of God's plan for salvation.***

In Chapter 20, Part IV of the Text is found the following information totally supportive of Workbook Lesson #98

*Paragraph 8. . . . But ask yourself if it is possible for God to have a plan for your salvation that does not work. **Once you accept His plan as the one function you would fulfill, there will be nothing else the Holy Spirit will not arrange for you without your effort. He will go before you*** *making straight your path, and leaving in your way no stones to trip on, and no obstacles to bar your way. Nothing you need will be denied you. Not one seeming difficulty but will melt away before you reach it. You need take thought for nothing, careless of everything except the only purpose that you would fulfill. As that was given you, so will its fulfillment be. God's guarantee will hold against all obstacles, for it rests on certainty and not contingency. It rests on you. And what can be more certain than a Son of God?*

A Course in Miracles—Manual for Teachers— an Introduction.

As I mentioned earlier when describing how I was introduced to *ACIM, the Manual for Teachers* was my entering point. In recent years I have led discussion groups studying *ACIM*. In one of the discussion groups I facilitated I used the following to stimulate discussion:

A PHILOSOPHY FOR TEACHERS

You can't not be a teacher and you can't not be a student. You will either be an excellent teacher and student, a mediocre one or a poor one. It is a matter of personal choice and effort! [Not from *ACIM*]

PART 1. WHO ARE GOD'S TEACHERS?

Excerpts from *The Manual for Teachers*

Page 3, Par 1 *A teacher of God is anyone who chooses to be one. His qualifications consist solely of this. . . . Once he has done that, his road is established. . . . He has entered an agreement with God. . . .*

Par 2, *They come from all over the world. They come from all religions and from no religion. . . . The Call is universal. . . . Many hear It, but few will answer. . . .*

Par 4, *This is a manual for a special curriculum intended for teachers of a special form of the universal course. There are thousands of other forms, all with the same outcome.*

PART 2. WHO ARE THE PUPILS?

Page 5, Par 1. *Certain pupils have been assigned to each of God's teachers, and they will begin to look for him as soon as he has answered the Call.*

Par 4, *The pupil comes at the right time to the right place. This is inevitable because he made the right choice in that ancient instant which he now relives.*

Page 6, Par 5. *When pupil and teacher come together, a teaching-learning situation begins. For the teacher is not really the one who does the teaching. God's Teacher [the Holy Spirit] speaks to any two who join together for learning purposes.*

PART 4. WHAT ARE THE CHARACTERISTICS OF GOD'S TEACHERS?

Excerpts From the 10 Characteristics:

I Trust

Par. 1 *This is the foundation on which their ability to fulfill their function rests. . . . The teachers of God have trust in the world, because they have learned it is not governed by laws the world made up. It is governed by a power that is in them but not of them.*

Par. 2 *When this power has been experienced, it is impossible to trust one's own petty strength again.*

Par. 6 *Yet when he (the teacher) is ready to go on, he goes with mighty companions [Spirit guides and Angels] beside him.*

II Honesty

Par. 1 *All other traits of God's teachers rest on trust. Once that has been achieved, the others cannot fail to follow. Only the trusting can afford honesty. . . . The term actually means consistency. . . . At no level are they in conflict with themselves . . . it is impossible for them to be in conflict with anyone or anything.*

III Tolerance

Par. 1 *God's teachers do not judge. To judge is to be dishonest, for to judge is to assume a position you do not have. No teacher of God can judge and hope to learn.*

IV Gentleness

Par. 1 *Harm is impossible for God's teachers. . . harm can actually achieve nothing.*

Par, 2 *Therefore God's teachers are wholly gentle. They need the strength of gentleness. . . .*

V Joy

Par 1. *Joy is the result of gentleness. Gentleness means that fear is now impossible. . . . Joy goes with gentleness as surely as grief attends attack.*

VI Defenselessness

Par, 1 *God's teachers have learned how to be simple. Their joy comes from understanding Who created them. . . . No one can become an advanced teacher of God until he understands that defenses are foolish guardians of mad illusions . . . it is not danger that comes when defenses are laid down. It is safety. It is peace. It is joy. And it is God.*

VII Generosity

Par. 1 *. . . To the teachers of God, it means giving away in order to keep . . . alien to the thinking of the world.*

Par. 2 *The teacher of God is generous out of Self interest. . . . The teacher of God does not want anything he cannot give away. . . .*

VIII Patience

Par, 1 *Those who are certain of the outcome can afford to wait, and to wait without anxiety. Patience is natural to the teacher of God. . . . All he sees is certain outcome . . . not in doubt. . . . Patience is natural to those who trust.*

IX Faithfulness

Par. 1 . . . *Faithfulness is the teacher of God's trust in the Word of God to set all things right; not some, but all.*

X Open-Mindedness

Par. 1 *Open-mindedness comes with lack of judgment. As judgment shuts the mind against God's Teacher, so open-mindedness invites Him to come in. . . . Only the open-minded can be at peace. . . .*

Par. 2 . . . *Forgiveness is the final goal of the curriculum.*

AN EXERCISE FOR THE COMMITTED TEACHER OF GOD

The following chart provides a self-help tool that can help a T O G, (teacher of God) become more competent.

"HOW AM I DOING?"

CHARACTERISTICS OF AN EXCELLENT TEACHER AND STUDENT

THE 10 "BEs" of an excellent student and teacher

INSTRUCTIONS: RATE YOURSELF PERIODICALLY FOR INCREASED SELF-AWARENESS

Code: '–' Needs Attention; '+' Some Progress; '++' Satisfactory

THE 10 "BEs" of an excellent student and teacher				
Characteristic	Date/ Rating	Date/ Rating	Date/ Rating	Date/ Rating
BE Trusting				
BE Honest				
BE Tolerant				
BE Gentle				
BE Joyful				
BE Defenseless				
BE Generous				
BE Patient				
BE Faithful				
BE Open-Minded				

OTHER ESSAYS RELATED TO *A COURSE IN MIRACLES:*

THE PARABLE OF THE RED DRESS

Gloria arose early and began her day by dressing for the most important meeting of her professional career. The advertising company she founded twenty-five years earlier was flourishing. On this much anticipated day she was meeting with the board of directors of a potential new client. If she and her assistant were successful in landing a contract it would be, by far, the largest in her career. She was genuinely excited but not fearful.

As she was preparing for the big day she removed two of her favorite dresses from her closet—a green one and a red one. Both dresses were designed for a professional woman and she found them equally attractive.

She stood in front of a full length mirror as she held up each dress to help in her decision making. She asked the question, *"Which one feels better?"* Very quickly she became aware that the green one felt better.

Gloria had no way of knowing that the president of the board of directors had a strong negative bias about any woman who wore red.

During the meeting Gloria and her assistant were treated with attention, dignity and respect. The president and the board were very pleased with the presentation and unanimously agreed to a lucrative, long term contract.

During the next several months Gloria and her employees met frequently with representatives of the new client. The respect and admiration for Gloria and her team reflected the quality and effectiveness of their advertising campaign. Six months into the contract the president was so impressed with the results that he scheduled a formal dinner to honor Gloria and her team.

On that fateful evening as Gloria dressed for the occasion the red dress felt better. She wore it. The bias the president had against women wearing red was changed forever.

If you so choose, God's voice will speak to you throughout the day without interrupting your regular activities in any way. ACIM

GRANDMA HAM'S WISDOM

One beautiful Indian summer day, when I was a small boy of nine or ten years, Grandma Ham and I were sitting in rocking chairs on her porch. Our family had recently gone through a family crisis. In her best story telling style she told me, *"Buddy, life is like a mountain river; sometimes it runs still and smooth, deep and peaceful. But you can be sure that downstream a bit there will be rapids and perhaps even falls. And then it will smooth out again for a time. Our challenge is to accept whatever the river of life hands us, doing our best and always knowing we are never left alone and comfortless by our Creator. We should always remember—this too, shall pass."*

THE RIVER OF LIFE

Life is analogous to a river that each of God's children, born into life on earth, **has chosen to experience.** Firstly, let us accept that the River of Life knows where it is going! If this becomes a "knowing" (stronger than a belief) it is an easily made decision *to go with the flow!* Because of our earth-bound educations, unless we accept this knowing most human beings become "human doings" and resist or fight against the currents of life. Our human directed educations teach us to deal with life's adversities by overcoming them by whatever means or energy it takes, thereby giving validity to the problem.

It is very useful for us to understand that every time we have chosen to view a life event as a problem **we can choose again!** If I accept an event as a problem it is adversarial to my best interests and I must defeat it, often times at great expense of energy, time and material resources. If I accept the event as a lesson, *from which I can learn,* the event is a blessing.

The unwanted event is analogous to a large rock in The River of Life. The rock or barrier is my opportunity to use the resource of Divine Guidance and have a positive learning experience rather than an event reducing the joy in my life.

As we travel down life's river we can "go with the flow" with a minimum of effort and enjoy greater peace and true quality of life. As we go down life's river with a minimum of effort—going with the flow rather than paddling upstream another lesson from the *ACIM WORKBOOK* will prove useful:

Lesson 50–*I am sustained by the love of God. Only the love of God will protect you in all circumstances. It will lift you out of every trial, and raise you high above all the perceived dangers of this world into a climate of perfect peace and safety.*

A PHILOSOPHY OF DEATH

A few years ago my oldest daughter called me and asked in a plaintive manner, "Dad, what am I going to do when you die?" My response was, "You will probably cry and be sad for a while and even though you miss me you will get on with life." She said, "That's easy for you to say because you have developed a philosophy. Please write one for me." I did and it follows:

A PHILOSOPHY OF DEATH

An adequate philosophy of life must include a philosophy of death.

We are born unequal

✧ Some are born into wealth some into poverty

✧ Some with beautiful, strong healthy and functional bodies and minds, some with lesser

We live unequal.

✧ Some live many years, some only a short time

✧ Some seem to accomplish much, some very little

✧ Some would describe their lives as happy, some as unhappy

✧ Some die easy without pain, some die hard with great pain

Death is the only equal event in life.

✧ There are no failures, everyone succeeds

✧ Our physical bodies are left behind, pain filled or painless

✧ Even the wealthiest person leaves this life without a possession

Some believe all of life is an accident—"chance" not "design." My thinking, investigation and learning has led me to a different conclusion. There are no accidents. There is order in all of nature. There is also purpose. We are well advised to ask: *"What is my purpose?"* We have been taught that there is a simple test to determine whether or not our purpose in life is finished— if we are here it isn't.

We are born unequal and are therefore unequal in our being—***by the standards of the world!*** In short, the world's standards for a life well lived are wealth, status, prestige and appearances. Spiritual teaching admonishes us: *Never compare yourself to others because your life's path is unique only to you. It is therefore ill-advised to compare your history of this life with anyone else's.*

Yet, we have a common purpose: ***To become as much as we can with our uniqueness, our strengths and our deficiencies. To discover as many truths as we can from all available*** *sources, especially the events in our lives— the beautiful AND the ugly. Every event contains a lesson. If we learn the lesson <u>every</u> event is a gift and we will <u>never</u> be a victim. An equally important purpose is to help others become as much as they can.*

Our life is a school and we cannot consciously know, in advance, what lessons we are here to learn. As previously stated, the spiritual message is that **every** event in life has a lesson God would have us learn. If we benefit from the event *it will be because we have* **chosen** *to do so!* Thus, problems become gifts. Our free will is never impinged. Therefore, victimhood is a choice **and we can choose differently!**

The widely accepted axiom—*As you sow, so shall you reap*—confirms that there is no such thing as something for nothing. We live in a world of cause and effect—karma. There is justice and being born unequal is part of that justice.

I do not believe in the concept of hell. Rather, I accept the first tenant of the Spiritualist Church which reads: *The door to reformation or oneness with God is never closed to any human soul here or hereafter.*

When our mission is finished there is no purpose to live longer in this incarnation. There is no such thing as an untimely death.

The Rest of the Story

For nearly 20 years I wrote and published a monthly learning resource "news letter" for my dentist clients. Soon after I had written the first draft of *A Philosophy of Death* a dear client friend died. I included in the paper a memorial piece about my friend and included the essay on death. Shortly after the letter went out I received a letter from Dr. Harold Wirth, who lived in New Orleans.

At that time, by almost any estimate, Dr. Wirth was one of the most loved and respected dentists in the world. In his letter he thanked me for writing about what he referred to as, "Man's final achievement." And he thanked me for my contributions to the dental profession and thanked me for being his mentor! When I read that I wept.

ADDITIONAL INFORMATION FROM ACIM I HAVE FOUND USEFUL

TAKING ANOTHER SHOT AT LUCIFER—THE DEVIL

The greatest fear for many people is fear of the evil one, the devil. The greatest sham; the greatest rationalization (cop out) in humankind's history is to blame any evil or mean-spirited behavior on the devil. Yes, there is evil in the world but it is invariably caused by man. When people blame evil, fear-based behavior on an external force—the devil—they are denying responsibility for their behavior and he or she has placed a great barrier to his or her growth—the evil was ego driven!

To fear the devil is to fear ourselves and to believe God is impotent. Evil has no power man does not give it.

A Course in Miracles, a very practical guide to love-based living states: **believing in the devil doesn't make any sense.**

ACIM–TEXT, PAGE 209, CHAPTER 11, PART VI, PARAGRAPHS 9 AND 10

> EXCERPTS: Par 9– . . . *You must see the works I do through you, or you will not perceive that I have done them unto you. Do not set limits on what I can do through you or you will not accept what I can do for you.*

> Par 10– . . . *For your part must be like mine if you learn it of me. If you believe that yours is limited you are limiting mine. . . . The whole power of God is in every part of Him . . . And to Christ it is given to be like the Father.*

ACIM WORKBOOK–LESSON 98

> *I will accept my part of God's plan for salvation.*

> Excerpts: Par 1– *In gladness we accept it as it is, and take the part assigned by God.*

> Par 2–*We have a mighty purpose to fulfill, and have been given everything we need with which to reach the goal. . . . All our sins have been washed away by realizing they were but mistakes.*

One of the lessons in the workbook has the following four questions recommended for starting each day:

1. *Father God what would you have me do today?*
2. *Where would you have me go today?*
3. *What would you have me say today?*
4. *To whom would you have me say it?*

With great respect for the above four questions I have chosen to add a fifth one to my ritual for beginning each day:

5. *What would you have me think today?*

Chapter Seven

THE JESHUA LETTERS AND THE WAY OF MASTERY

A FEW YEARS AGO I became aware that a small group of people in the Denver area met every Sunday morning and studied *A Course in Miracles*. The organization is The Rocky Mountain Miracle Center. I began attending "The Gathering," as they called it, on Sunday mornings. Each Sunday one of several teachers facilitated a discussion about some excerpts from the *Course*. After about 25 years of independently studying *ACIM* I found the camaraderie quite enjoyable and the discussions enlightening.

One Sunday I noticed a group of people leaving the Center about the time The Gathering started. A few from that group joined The Gathering. I was told that the group I hadn't noticed before came an hour earlier and it was also a study club. I decided to come an hour earlier the next time I visited and find out what it was all about. I felt quite sure it was another ACIM study group. I was wrong. They were studying another book, *The Way of Mastery*.

To my knowledge all of the people who had gathered to study and discuss *The Way of Mastery* were also students of *A Course in Miracles.* Many of them consider *The Way of Mastery* as a sequel or follow-up to *ACIM. It was published about 20 years later in the 1990s.*

This course of study was delivered in a somewhat similar fashion as *ACIM*—dictated by Jesus. This time the scribe was an accountant living in Seattle, Washington, Jon Marc Hammer. He too, just as with Helen Schucman, the scribe for ACIM, was quite reluctant at first and resisted being the scribe. He was told the messenger he was receiving from was Jeshua ben Joseph, otherwise known as Jesus.

The messages from Jeshua, channeled through Jon Marc, were first published as *The Jeshua Letters*. That book is available through Amazon.com. This smaller book introduced me to *The Way of Mastery* described below.

Following the delivery of *The Jeshua Letters,* there was one channeled message per month for 35 consecutive months. Most of them are about one hour in length and are now available on audio CDs from T*he Shanti Christo Foundation.* These sessions were tape recorded and later transcribed. During this dictation Jeshua frequently refers to his previous book, *A Course in Miracles.*

Three parts to the book were communicated in this manner: *The Way of the Heart; The Way of Transformation* and *The Way of Knowing.* These three parts have been combined into one volume with the title, *The Way of Mastery.* The book and the CDs are available from the Shanti Christo Foundation, a non-profit organization. Their website is www.shantichristo.org. It is with great thanks to Shanti Christo for the opportunity to share the following life changing, paraphrased information.

After mentally devouring and deeply appreciating *The Jeshua Letters* I obtained a copy of *The Way of Mastery.* I have found that, for me, it clarifies and therefore strengthens many of the important messages contained in *ACIM.*

PART ONE:

THE WAY of the HEART

A FEW OF THE LEARNINGS FROM
The Way of the Heart:

THE IMPORTANCE OF DESIRE—Lesson 4

The concept this lesson teaches is that all human initiated activity begins with desire. Certainly when we are thirsty or hungry we are motivated to satisfy that desire. In the case of physical needs we are sufficiently clear to do whatever is necessary.

We are also clear that the only absolute constant in our world is change. To be sure change in our worldly environment can have a major effect on what we desire. Sometimes changes in our worldly circumstances make it very clear that we need to consider personal changes. These situations can be labeled as times of *transition.* It is to our definite advantage, at such times, if we are as clear as possible on what we really, really desire.

The following four step process, from Lesson 4, can be very helpful:

✧ *DESIRE*—Be maximally clear on what you desire.

✧ *INTENTION*—Develop an action plan.

✧ *ALLOW*—If an action step doesn't work it's not a failure.

✧ *SURRENDER*—Ask for Devine guidance.

DESIRE Step one

For seven mornings, after you are fully awake but before you start your day, on a note pad write the date and then answer the following question: "At this time what do I really, really want." List seven items. Place the lists in a drawer and do not refer back to them until you have done this seven times.

Review the seven lists and "batch" them or categorize them. For example several of the listed desires may relate to the same subject. Next prioritize them; decide which desire or desires you will concentrate on first and develop your next step.

INTENTION Step two

This is the action step. **The intention activity will be much more effective because of the strength of clarified desire.** It is recommended that you think through and continuously ask for guidance as you develop your plan. An intention is an **objective.**

By definition an objective is:
1. Definitely attainable
2. Very specific
3. Measureable
4. Sort range
5. Announced time frame

ALLOW Step three

This important component of our thinking/planning/ action efforts assures that there will be no **failure—just something that didn't work.** If an action doesn't work it is a stepping stone toward what will work! What did I learn from that effort? Don't give up!

To allow is the opposite of judging. This concept has far reaching benefits. *One who cultivates the ability to allow is cultivating, in truth, the very act of forgiveness.* [TWOM page 253] It is well to be aware that anything I resist I am judging.

SURRENDER Step four

If you have not previously done so, submit/surrender all of your process to the Holy Spirit for His purposes and ask for continued guidance. Record any thoughts that you have following the act of surrendering. *Be aware, this activity can change your life.*

GUIDING AXIOMS (Excerpted from Lessons 2 and 3)
✧ *I am created as my Father created me to be. I am free. And nothing sources my experience in each moment. Nothing has an effect upon me whatsoever, save that which I choose to allow to affect me.*

✧ *I need do nothing.*

✧ *I do not live in any ordinary moments. With each breath, my experiences are the stepping stones laid before me of God to guide me home. I will bring awareness to each moment and allow it to teach me how to forgive, how to embrace, how to love and therefore how to live fully.*

THE IMPORTANCE OF FORGIVENESS

It is widely accepted among students of ACIM that understanding forgiveness and developing the ability to practice it is a primary objective of the Course. This theme is furthered and reinforced in TWOM and is obvious in the above third axiom. Additionally from TWOM:

✧ *Judgment is a [painful] contraction.*

✧ *Forgiveness is relaxation, peace, trust and faith.*

✧ *Judgment causes every cellular structure to break down. If you could see this you would never judge again.* [The strength of our immune system plunges.]

It is critically important that we forgive others for our perception of their "wrong doing" and that we forgive ourselves for judging them.

From ACIM *"when we judge we are assuming an ability we do not have." We never have all of the pertinent facts and we cannot know what happens in the future.*

Forgiveness, itself, becomes a delightful energy to live within.

THE IMPORTANCE OF CLOSING OUT EACH DAY

It is very, very important to let each day be sufficient unto itself. [Before sleep] *I release this day. It has been perfect and it is done.*

Medical Intuitive, Carolyn Myss: "If we do not release the past our biology will be affected by our biography."

THE IMPORTANCE OF HUMILITY

No single characteristic is of greater importance than humility—not the feigned humility that is taught in certain world religions, but a genuine humility.

Genuine humility flows from a deep-seated recognition that you cannot save yourself. . . . [And as previously written, *Of myself I can do nothing but the Father working through me . . .*]

NOTE: As this is being written I am 82 years old. I have been a student of *A Course in Miracles* for 30 years and a student of *The Way of Mastery* for 7 years. Studying and working with this spiritual path has profoundly influenced my life. I live with significantly more peace and less fear than I thought possible. Without question, the most powerfully life altering activity has been accepting my divinity as described below.

Celebrate Your Re-birth as Christ
Lesson 10 Page 131

. . . simply choose a date—approximately seven weeks in the future—signifying for your day of re-birth. Let each day be seen as a step, a pilgrimage, a completion of a very ancient circle. Let each day be one in which you reaffirm your commitment to releasing everything unlike Love in yourself, so that as you come to your appointed day, you will dedicate yourself to being prepared for it.

On the eve of your chosen day, go to bed early enough and in quiet and in prayer, so that you can awaken before the first rays of the new day come to caress the earth.

Take yourself outdoors, even if you must bundle up the body. Make haste to a place of vision . . . [For me it was in a lake park, a natural setting.]

There, turn to face the direction of the arising sun, and go into a simple prayer. Realize that you see nothing through the physical eyes anyway. Stand with the arms at the sides with the palms open. Breathe deeply into the body, relax the mind, and begin simply to say within yourself:

> *Death has occurred, and now the birth of Christ is at hand. Father, I accept fully your will for me. Your will is only that I be happy and use time to extend my treasure. Now, I receive the warmth of your Light and your Love.*

Then merely stand and wait, and receive the warmth of the light.

Now the journey to the Kingdom is over and the journey within it can begin.

When you journey back to your home on that morning, do something to celebrate your birth day. As (your name) the Christ.

. . . It is time to birth fully the presence of the peaceful Christ within you.

In the King James version of The Holy Bible, when discussing miracles, Jesus said; *"And greater things than these shall you do."*

NOTE: I pondered long about the appropriateness of including this life altering event in this writing.

I followed the recommendation I frequently make to coaching clients: **Ask for guidance!**

I am quite well aware that the above described activity will cause many different reactions from readers and listeners, many of whom are dearly beloved Brothers and Sisters and devout Christians. I suspect these reactions will vary from complete rejection—to wonderment—all the way to, "Wow, maybe I should consider my divinity."

A DECLARATION OF FAITH

Recently I was asked by a person with whom I was sharing my opinions, attitudes, beliefs and *"knowings"* as a spiritual coach. He asked how I would respond to another person if they asked, "Bud, are you a Christian." The question touched me deeply.

I responded, after a short term assessment, by saying, "By the definition of a Christian by some of my fundamentalist Christian friends I do not qualify." I quickly added: "Jesus, (whose Jewish name, perhaps more correctly rendered is Jeshua Ben Joseph) is my best friend, my spiritual mentor and master. We entered into a partnership almost 20 years ago. [As reported in my book *CHANGING PLACES*.] I talk to him many times each day and to my satisfaction he talks to me."

I have been a student of contemporary spiritual teaching for somewhat over 50 years. I believe every spiritual seeker wants the most accurate understanding possible about our relationship with God. The approach I have been studying for the past 30 plus years is often referred to as "New Age." This is often seen to as blasphemy by those who believe the Bible is the actual and final word/teaching of our Creator. I do not believe God stopped trying to help us 2000 years ago.

By my definition I am most definitely a Christian.

PART TWO:

THE WAY of TRANSFORMATION
AN OVERVIEW

A FEW OF MY LEARNINGS FROM
The Way of Transformation:

A REQUIREMENT IS TO COMMIT TO LIVING DIFFERENTLY, CHAPTER 13, PAGE157.

The Way of Transformation absolutely requires that you be committed to living differently. . . . One thing and one thing only will bring you into the transformation you have sought—the willingness to abide where you are, differently.

TRANSFORMATION IS MORE OF A CHANGE OF ATTITUDE RATHER THAN A CHANGE OF CIRCUMSTANCES

It is imperative for us to realize that the greatest control we have over our lives is **our thoughts.** As reported earlier in this writing, fear-based, and mean-spirited thoughts create defeatist attitudes and come to all of us! **But they cannot serve us well.** *"I can choose again!!"*

A MAJOR TRANSFORMATION IS CONTINUOUSLY EXTENDING LOVE FOR ONLY LOVE IS REAL

ACIM and TWOM repeatedly point out that the only constant in *our* world is change. Love is of God, not of the world and is the only thing that never changes —everything birthed in time is referred to as "illusion" and will pass away.

EMPHASIS ON THE TRUISM
"I AND MY FATHER ARE ONE"

I and my Father are one. There is nothing I need to do to <u>get</u> God. There are only some things to be released, so that God <u>can get me.</u> TWOM page 177

IT IS OUR CHOICE TO LIVE IN LOVE OR FEAR

To live with more love and its attendant emotions is very simple—it depends on making love-based, rather than fear-based, decisions. Just ask, "What would Jesus do?"

THE ULTIMATE IN TOLERANCE IS TO ACCEPT ALL
THINGS WITHOUT JUDGMENT—TO "ALLOW"

If you have not read Ekhart Tolle's books *A New Earth* or *The Power of Now,* I highly recommend them. To master *allowing* is one of the most difficult traits we ego driven humans can develop. To "allow" something does not mean that we condone it. Allowing is the opposite of judgment. It is well for us to remember that intolerance leads to judgment; judgment leads to prejudice—the monumental contributing factor to human strife and suffering. Without prejudice we would have no wars.

PART THREE:

THE WAY of KNOWING

AN OVERVIEW

A FEW OF THE LEARNINGS FROM
The Way of Knowing

GOD AND I ARE ONE
AND CANNOT BE SEPARATED

Throughout TWOM many paragraphs begin with:
I and my Father are one. . . . (a few of the following statements)

❖ *Of myself I can do nothing but the Father working through me accomplishes all good things.*

❖ *Only Love is real. I cannot possibly be a victim of what I see, since I see what I choose to see. . . .*

❖ *Only Love is real, and Love alone heals. . . .*

❖ *I am that which I am.*

❖ *I am intimately connected with that very Source from which all things have sprung forth.*

EVERY HUMAN BEING IS MY BROTHER
OR MY SISTER

It doesn't matter whether you accept it or not—it is as it is—no matter your color, your nationality, gender, spirituality or lack of, or sexual preference. Please consider how this would impact quality of life on earth if every person accepted this. **It is indeed a rare person who would intentionally harm a brother or sister!**

RE-EMPHASIS ON A VERY IMPORTANT KEY TO THE KINGDOM—*ALLOWANCE* OF ALL EVENTS RATHER THAN JUDGMENT

As previously presented in this writing if we master the concept of *allowing* we need not be concerned about forgiveness because we will have avoided judgment! Let us keep in mind that to resist anything is to judge it. It is also important to remember that to allow does not mean condoning.

WHEN WE SEE A BROTHER OR SISTER WE SEE CHRIST

You are also looking at Christ when you look in the mirror! Please try to imagine how you will feel when (not if) you accept this! The following is in the introduction to **A Course In Miracles:**

It is a required course. Only the time you take is voluntary.

THE MAJOR PURPOSE OF MY LIFE IS TO BE A CONDUIT FOR LOVE

Your path in this incarnation is totally unique—it has never been experienced by any other soul—be assured **you do have a specific mission!** If you exhibit *"A little willingness"* (from ACIM) and a desire to know your mission, *you will know* your part of God's plan.

LOVE IS FREEDOM AND FREEDOM AND LOVE CANNOT BE SEPARATED

Unconditional love requires unconditional freedom. If we master **allowing**—the opposite of judgment—it is assured forgiveness is unnecessary.

A PARTING SHOT

A s you may have gathered from this writing I am
one who knows that God is in charge of His
universe—there are no accidents—there is no death—
there are no chance meetings—therefore there are no
victims. The world is unfolding just as it is supposed
to. You and I will have more peace in our futures if
we adopt the choice of *ALLOWING,* rather than judging and *LOVING* rather than fearing. It is my desire
for this book to contribute to that process.

Index

Journal

www.ingramcontent.com/pod-product-compliance
Lightning Source LLC
Chambersburg PA
CBHW071553040426
42452CB00008B/1163